# WHEN THE WORLD WAS YOUNG

# WHEN THE WORLD WAS YOUNG

A COMPANION VOLUME TO THE GRANADA TV SERIAL

# LOST EMPIRES

Graham Nown

WARD LOCK LIMITED · LONDON
IN ASSOCIATION WITH
GRANADA TELEVISION

First published in Great Britain in 1986
by Ward Lock Limited, 8 Clifford Street,
London W1X 1RB, an Egmont Company.

Designed by Melissa Orrom
Text filmset in Bembo by
Dorchester Typesetting Group Ltd.

Printed and bound in Spain by Graficas Reunidas

**British Library Cataloguing in Publication Data**

Nown, Graham
  When the world was young.
  1. Music-halls (Variety-theaters, cabarets,
  etc.)—History 2. Vaudeville—History
  I. Title
  792.7'09          PN1962

  ISBN 0-7063-6484-8

**Endpapers:** *Popularity. Stars of the Music Hall.*
Oil Painting by Walter Lambert, 1901-1903.

# CONTENTS

# THE LOST
# SUMMER

A glorious week by the sea.

COKETOWN FIVE AM: cold water splashes on slop-stones; the knocker-up rattles on windows hung with faded drapes; coughs and wheezes; steaming kettles; spits and groans; the first tram's galvanizing clang. A curtain of sulphurous smoke hangs heavily over dark rows of back-to-backs as sounds repeated all over the North rise in a reluctant symphony.

Life for Britain's working millions had a monotonous regularity before World War I. Along mean, cobbled streets lay anything up to twelve hours of backbreaking work and punishing discomfort. Foundries which numbed the eardrums, mills which filled the lungs with cotton dust, and factories which left a taste in the mouth that even a whole Sunday on the moors could not remove.

On the surface there was little to laugh about, but an air of chumminess, a dash of naïve optimism and an odd hope that everything would turn out all right, characterized life in the streets. The dark satanic mills bred a chirpy cynicism which produced half a century of popular heroes like Billy Bennett, George Formby and Gracie Fields.

Days were long, factory output high and working people had precious little leisure; but the headlong way they chose to spend it summed up their attitude to life. For a glorious week each year the industrial towns of England were deserted by families hellbent on sea air, beer and high living. Excursion trains deposited them on the platforms of Bridlington and Scarborough with suitcases and bundles – an army of displaced persons with bright eyes, hollow coughs and rickety legs.

There were quiet resorts favoured by the elderly, resorts famed for their bracing ozone, and a few which reverberated to the late-night sound of breaking glass. But the queen of them all, the jewel of the North West coast, where the sewage met the sea, was big, brassy Blackpool. Despite the comic postcard landladies who crammed them in, silent dinners spent fumbling with soup-spoons, and the surcharge for use of the cruet, Blackpool had everything.

In wakes week, when excursion trains plied nose-to-tail across the Pennines and the Lancashire plain, overcrowding was rife. The *Rochdale Observer* satirized the typical Blackpool landlady: 'Last summer we were rather pushed,' she says, 'so I fitted a board over the scullery sink for two youngsters to sleep on, and swung a hammock in the cellar steps with a breadth of carpet and the clothes line – it was the coolest place in the house, so I charged sixpence extra for it . . .'

Before World War I well-scrubbed coal and cotton families could imitate the boss by lounging in an upholstered landau down the prom. They heckled eminent thespians in the resort's palatial theatres (a tradition begun years earlier when Sarah Bernhardt decided enough was enough and stormed off-stage because voices from the gods were calling, 'Speak up lass – we can't hear a word!') And, for a fee, they could stand in awe in the Winter Gardens where the management invited them to 'spit on Bill Holland's hundred guinea carpet.' After a few beers miners' wives would slip off their shoes on the sands and knit, while their husbands played porrin' – kicking each other's shins until one of them fell down.

Donkey rides along the sands.

And, of course, there was the famous Tower, a 158 m (520 ft) maroon finger pointing at the dull, pudding-bag clouds drifting ominously overhead. No one in Blackpool really heeded the weather – 'golden showers' the mayor called them, to publicize the vast assortment of entertainments under one roof huddled around the foot of the Tower. At the centre of it all was the Ballroom, glittering in over 4500 litres (1000 gallons) of peach and gold paint and 6,750 books of gold leaf. Couples could walk on deep carpets, glide on a floor mounted on springs surrounded by marble pillars and sweeping balconies, and gaze at the vaulted ceiling decorated with a gallery of garish frescoes. At the end of a bloated day of chips and beer, Blackpool knew how to turn on the romance.

Blackpool Pier.

IMAGES OF the Edwardian era, however, are generally far removed from such rough-and-ready realism. They are usually rich and colourful – a slow-paced world of picture hats and parasols, summer lawns and elegant living – viewed through a gauze of nostalgia like a Sickert painting. Each in its own way was a different side of the English coin. But the most vivid and enduring of all memories was that of 1914, when both the rich on their croquet lawns and the poor in their back-yards, enjoyed a heatwave.

Much has been written of that idyllic summer. There were times when it seemed to stretch forever, and the sun would never stop shining over England. From early April until the end of June less than half an inch of rain was recorded at King's Somborne, Hampshire, as the hot weeks rolled into one another. Wheat and barley were harvested early in record crops, leaving sentry-rows of sheaves shimmering in an endless landscape of stubble.

Even in London, where office workers fingered their stiff collars and sweltered in 34°C (94°F) on 1 July, the pace slowed. Parks were full of parasols and strolling girls in summer dresses. Small pleasure craft murmured in their hundreds on the Thames. In the evenings, laughter and ragtime music croaking from wind-up gramophones filled the balmy riverbank air.

If a maiden means to marry
On a houseboat she should tarry,
And a man she's sure to catch;
For the picnics and the dances
Will afford her endless chances
To bring him to the scratch!

For when the moon is mellow
Up on deck she takes the fellow
Whom she thinks she wants to wed,
And she flirts with him reclining
In a blouse that lacks a lining,
And he's bound to lose his head.

Wheat and barley were harvested early in record crops.

The rich and famous took to the water in mahogany and brass steam launches, sporting naval caps at jaunty angles. Along the Thames businesses blossomed, often with obscure rules which semaphored that riff-raff in rowing boats were not required. *Punch* impishly recorded this variety song about one of the snobbish new establishments:

> There's a river hotel that is known very
>   well,
> From the turmoil of London withdrawn,
> Between Henley and Staines, where this
>   strange rule obtains
> That you must not eat jam on the lawn.
>
> In the coffee room still you may eat what
>   you will,
> Such as chicken, beef, mutton and brawn,
> Jam and marmalade, too; but, whatever
>   you do,
> Don't attempt to eat jam on the lawn.

> Young Jones and his bride sought the cool
>   riverside,
> And she said, as she skipped like a faun
> 'As it is, it is nice, but t'would be paradise
> Could we only eat jam on he lawn' . . .

The Earl of Stockton, an Oxford under-graduate in that long, hot summer, re-membered how suddenly the world changed. 'The First War burst like a bombshell on ordinary people,' he recalled in *Winds of Change*. 'It came suddenly and unexpectedly – a real bolt from the blue . . . Indeed in the summer of 1914 there was far more anxiety about a civil war in Ireland than about a world war in Europe. Certainly, had we been told, when we were enjoying the carefree life of Oxford in the summer term of 1914, that in a few weeks all our little band of friends would abandon for ever academic life and rush to take up arms, still more, that only a

Small pleasure craft murmured in their hundreds on the Thames.

A vogue for glittering fancy
dress parties seized the rich.

few were destined to survive a four years' conflict, we should have thought such prophecies the ravings of a maniac. . .'

No era in modern times has ended quite so abruptly. It was, indeed, the end of an empire, a lost age which has no place in the modern world. Queen Victoria's stern standards had faded with her funeral in 1901 – a suitably sombre spectacle with the coffin borne, gently bobbing, on the deck of the Royal yacht. In an end befitting an empress, it steamed majestically down the Solent, shadowed by the grey might of the Navy.

Few ordinary people on that frosty January morning could have realized that they were standing at the crossroads of history. Wealthy Edwardians reacted with a sense of quiet relief and plunged themselves into a decade of pleasure-seeking which has rarely been paralleled for ex-

travagance. Society glittered with round after round of balls and banquets, each trying to top the other for sheer excess. The privileged who still recall those golden days remember it as an age of enchantment.

A vogue for glittering fancy dress parties seized the rich, who thought nothing of spending enough to keep a family for a year on elaborate costumes, or on the hire of an Arab stallion to make a dazzling entrance. Flamboyance extended to food, which became almost a national obsession among those who could afford to live well. Edward VII, a sporty ladies' man with the well-developed paunch of a voracious eater, set the pace for the leisured classes.

Socially, he had the brilliance – and the shape – of a 200-watt bulb, lighting up a Court previously dimmed by Victoria's oppressive love of formality. On an average day he could demolish with ease a twelve-course breakfast – pheasant stuffed with snipe, in turn stuffed with truffles, was a particular favourite – before embarking on a morning's golf or shooting. New faces began to appear in Court circles – industrialists, businessmen and bankers, a far cry from the creaking aristocrats who had surrounded the Queen a decade previously.

'To keep in, to keep going, members of Edwardian high society toiled harder than overworked clerks or warehousemen,' says Priestley in his affectionate study, *The Edwardians*. 'It was a dreadful nuisance, of course, but a fellow would have to go down to Cowes for the first week in August, then go up North to shoot the grouse or stalk the deer. A woman invited for a weekend at one of the great houses would have to take several large trunks, and then would have to be changing clothes – and always looking her best – half a dozen times a day. A free and easy life in theory, in practice it was more highly disciplined and more weary than the life of a recruit in the Life Guards.'

The rich indelibly stamped their image on the age, but the poor and under-privileged were becoming dissatisfied with their drab lives and the roles they were required to play. At the bottom of the social pyramid there was disenchantment, trade union unrest, resolute women fighting for their rights, and the first mass-produced consumer goods which widened further the gulf between the haves and have-nots.

The twentieth century had a difficult birth, leaving Edwardians of those uneasy years uncertain as to which age they belonged. They may have believed that Britain ruled the world, but few could say it with the conviction of twenty years earlier. The future, with war clouds looming over Europe, was filled with painful foreboding.

Edward VII died in 1910, but the years up to the war were still infused with the heady influence of his reign. The post-Edwardian party continued in full swing, with an awkward awareness that the host had taken his leave. The lost summers leading up to the war have a suspended quality. Across the abyss, people remember them with a brilliant intensity, like a long, golden garden party. The poignant reality was that the old order was dying, and the world would never be quite the same again.

THE POOR, as always, had troubles of their own, but there was, at least, a brief escape – a few hours of warmth and opulence in the gilt and velvet splendour of the Music Hall. Even the theatre had its own reminders of class with the wealthy in the stalls, the middle class in the circle and the workers in the gods. However, Priestley recalled from his youth that the atmosphere was radical – Variety was 'always for the poor against the rich.' For a while at least, harsh work and the fear of war could be swallowed in belly-laughs in those beautiful palaces of honest vulgarity. Once lost in illusion, the screaming billboards and worrying head-lines must have seemed little more than a dream. 'They were all laughing, all happy because they did not know what was really happening backstage,' says Ian Curteis who scripted *Lost Empires*. 'Likewise, they did not know what was happening next year – the war.'

Variety was loud and brassy, like a reliable Model-T, running on a non-stop diet of giggles and rumbustious fun. There was possibly no time when the nation had a more real, almost desperate, hunger to be entertained. On rainy evenings in cavern-ous Alhambras and tin-roofed flea-pits, the second house was a heaving mass of humanity, warmed with beer, threadbare clothes gently steaming. An atmosphere of expectation, and a pervading smell of poverty. They had paid their money and were waiting to be entertained. And if they

They had paid their money and were waiting to be entertained.

Sir Laurence Olivier plays Harry Burrard.

weren't, then heaven help the artist who failed to tickle their fancy.

Priestley's broken-down comic Burrard in *Lost Empires* had lost the essential art of making 'em laugh. Laurence Olivier, who plays him with echoes of Archie Rice in *The Entertainer*, says in his *Confessions Of An Actor*: 'John Osborne has always maintained that the end of the Music Hall really did spell the end of our country's greatness. . . He claims, it seems to me with justification, that the one great property of the Music Hall was that through it could be clearly traced the tides of changing public taste. Every stand-up comedian relied to a great extend upon current topicalities; besides a liberal sprinkling of gossip of all kinds, politics provided the ripest field for comment. By noting the way in which these jokes were received – whether they brought the house down or misfired, or if indeed they were greeted with boos or hisses – the spectator, particularly if he happened to be a wide politician, could avail himself of this ready-to-hand testing ground, as could any student of social history.'

MUSIC HALL, Variety's predecessor, had evolved from London pubs and pleasure gardens to be patronized by all sides of society. In the early nineteenth century, shrewd landlords of the bigger taverns and saloons hired singers to entertain their customers. The atmosphere was noisy and smoke-filled – unlike grander theatres where smoking was banned and audiences listened to performances in silence. A few of these 'free-and-easies' were still around in Edwardian times, but were regarded as dinosaurs against the slickly evolving style of Variety.

Early music halls evolved from entertainment taverns which had become very popular among Victorians. Once admission fees were charged and more lavish bills assembled, the transition to Music Hall was almost complete. (There were inevitably untameable pockets of resistance, such as London's Pelican Tavern, forced to close when 'it's premises were stormed, and taken, by the Salvation Army.')

These early music halls were run by hard-headed businessmen who set out to pack in as many customers as the law would allow. Flock wallpaper, velvet curtains and gilt plasterwork were standard style in rich interiors. Leeds City Varieties had a Potato Room, where a constant supply of baked potatoes were cooked on an ancient black kitchen range behind the stalls. The aroma drifted through the theatre, adding to its cosy ambience. Many theatres had a Ladies Night when ladies accompanied by a gentleman were allowed in free. This led to crowds of girls blocking the pavement, hoping to lobby single men who might take them in. In the 'naughty nineties' London's Empire Theatre became a favourite place of business for 'ladies of the night', who touted for customers in the wide gangway behind the dress circle. When they began to rival the attractions on-stage, Mrs Ormiston Chant, the scourge of the music halls, and a forerunner of Mary Whitehouse, tried unsuccessfully to have the Empire's licence revoked.

In the early taverns, Mine Host announced the acts pounding the gavel he used to change his beer barrels, to keep order. When Music Hall moved to West End theatres and added dancers and novelty turns, he was replaced by a more restrained counterpart, familiar to viewers of TV's *The Good Old Days*. By the time Variety came along, the compère had been superceded by an easel on stage, displaying a card announcing the name of the act. Stage-hands changed them between turns, giving the show a quick-fire pace which was an essential part of its appeal.

Music hall stars, particularly the ladies,

Marie Lloyd, 'The Bernhardt of the music halls'.

were courted in high circles, and their performances regularly patronized by the raffish London well-to-do. It was the age of girls showing a well-turned ankle as they strutted Cockney songs. Marie Lloyd, perhaps the most celebrated of them all, soared from the Eagle Tavern, City Road, to the best theatres of the West End. 'The Bernhardt of the music halls', as she was dubbed, built her reputation on saucy songs with titles like *She'd Never Had Her Ticket Punched Before*. Marie always claimed that her stage philosophy was 'Cut it short is best – you can let them guess the rest'; but even in an age of strict morals, she left little to the imagination.

What's that for, eh! Oh tell me Ma
If you won't tell me, I'll ask Pa.
But Ma said, 'Oh, it's nothing, hold your
    row.'
Well, I've asked Johnny Jones, see,
So I know now!

Wracked by rheumatism, and fretting constantly over her fans who had deserted her for the cinema, Marie died on stage at the age of fifty-two. Characteristically, she was still singing – *One Of The Ruins That Cromwell Knocked About A Bit.*

Music Hall was rich in sauce and sentiment, and Albert Chevalier, The Coster Laureate, was a master of the mawkish ballad, with numbers such as *My Old Dutch*. Albert scribbled his hit on the back of an envelope as he walked from Oxford Street to Islington; and for the rest of his career he was not allowed to leave the stage without launching into

I've got a pal
A reg'lar out an' outer.
She's a dear good old gal,
I'll tell yer all about 'er. . .

Everyone in England had heard of Albert Chevalier, including the editor of the *Popular Phrenologist*, who despatched an investigative correspondent, Professor Swern, to examine the bumps on his head. Readers were given a detailed analysis of the great man, which concluded: 'His head is large – twenty-three inches in circumference measurement . . . One rarely examines an individual with so powerful a degree of Mirthfulness. . . Those fine human touches, given especially in his pathetic pieces and in his representations of old folk, are the products of an ingeniousness which is innate.' Albert was flattered by the tone of the article, but could not help observing: 'I wish he hadn't remarked about the size of my head. . .'

Music Hall was responsible for a wealth of talent, from the subtle clowning of Dan Leno to the vivacity of Marie Kendall, most of them now sadly forgotten save for a few scratchy gramophone recordings, or snatches of hand-cranked film. A few made the difficult transition to Variety, while others, by the arrival of the musical shows of the post-war years, had faded into retirement or obscurity. The West End theatres where they had once performed had switched to fast-paced shows which required stars to be on stage for long periods, singing and dancing. By then many were too old to summon the sheer physical stamina, and a new generation of bright young things took their place.

VARIETY, a rather less refined relative from out of town, had its roots firmly in the terraced streets and Lowry landscapes of the provinces. In the North, many of the bill-topping artists were on home ground and responded warmly to the cheers of their raggle-taggle army of supporters. 'I remember 'im when he was nowbut a lad,' must have been heard many times as they hurried for the last tram home.

Their heroes had escaped from the weaving sheds and coal mines to earn almost £1000 a week, ride in motor cars, and wear coats with astrakahn collars. No one begrudged them their success; indeed, there was a feeling among the families who queued to watch them that they had achieved it on their behalf. There was an innocent absence of the envy later generations might have felt. Fame was a commodity everyday folk had no desire to grapple with. They would have felt as awkward in astrakhan as ploughing through the tense silence of a boarding house breakfast. The greasepaint heroes from their own home town took away that awful need to succeed, and they went back to work the next day feeling all the better for it.

Riotous applause for bill-topping artists.

It explains, perhaps, the unique matey-ness between variety artists and their audiences, both off-stage and on. Right up until the days when the medium was struggling to survive, working people wanted to acknowledge their favourite stars, and expected the same in return. One old stage-hand tells a story of Frank Randle, the most outrageous and explosive comedian of them all, urinating against the wall of a Blackpool theatre as the last house made its way home. 'Goodnight Frank!' they called to the ex-miner from Wigan. 'Good neet!' waved Randle, holding back his cashmere coat with the other hand as he continued unabashed.

The theatre – and in some grim towns the term was loosely used – provided such a cocoon of comfort and security that there was a reluctance to leave. 'It was wonderful in a way to leave the darkening and chilly streets of Newcastle and then find oneself sitting in the fourth row at the Empire,' says Dick Herncastle in *Lost Empires*. 'I think the secret of all these music halls is that while they seemed big – and most of them were – at the same time they seemed warm, cosy, intimate.' In the tiny Lancashire hall where George Formby was to launch his career years later, a steady trickle of urine often meandered from the back of the house, down the tiered steps, to lap the central heating pipes at the foot of the stage. This peculiar problem – caused by an element who could not bear to miss even a few minutes of the show – made artists' eyes water, and prompted the elderly lady pianist to wear wellington boots beneath her floor-length evening gown. Small wonder, some remarked, that George had such a funny voice. . .

It was, perhaps, one of the penalties of being the greatest democratic form of entertainment. Variety catered for all classes and, while there were those who planted themselves firmly in their seats from the overture to the final curtain, others preferred the attractions of the bar to the more harrowing turns. Third-rate comedians, and sopranos who stretched for high notes with the desperation of the drowning clutching at a lifebelt, were among the unpopular acts known as bar-chasers. They were familiar to variety regulars, and many a beaming entrance was lost in a thunderous stampede for the exit.

Dick – and probably Priestley himself – was not impressed by some of the luke-warm talent which trod the boards. '. . . imbecile cross-talk comedians; boozy Irish tenors tearful over their mothers; "light comedians" with their endless songs about "girls with curly curls" and Brown and his pals out on a spree; the immensely popular but tedious male impersonators, who never once looked or sounded like the soldiers and sailors they were supposed to be impersonating. At least five acts out of every eight seemed to me to be a waste of anybody's attention. . .'

In some towns, particularly Glasgow's legendary houses, the first turn on the bill might be excused for feeling that he had been fed to the lions. By the time an act reached third or fourth spot, the welcome was inevitably warmer. An old trouper like Ganga Dun knew the wisdom of being the last act before the interval.

I N THE 1950s, when theatres had their seats ripped out to the beat of Bill Haley, and the acned lads of the Larry Parnes Stable, Variety was little more than a husk; a few dusty memories blowing in the corners of tarnished coliseums. A handful of jaded acts doggedly trod the boards of minor seaside towns, but the great tradition of the people's theatre had been swallowed by films and television and a mainstream of mediocrity.

Half a century earlier, Music Hall had been undergoing similar heartaches. As the world rumbled headlong into change, the whole field of entertainment was transforming as never before. Show business, popular magazines and sport were all acquiring a pace and sophistication geared to a mass audience eager for spectacle and excitement.

Transatlantic travel, despite the awesome Titanic tragedy of 1913, was faster and more frequent, bringing with it new ideas and fashions from ragtime America. This interchange of enthusiasm and imagination opened a floodgate of fads and foibles. Novelty in entertainment, art and engineering surpassed even the Victorians' wildest dreams.

No sooner had Britain tired of ping-pong and roller-skating, when along came Rose O'Neill, an unassuming American children's writer, who invented a chubby-faced character called Kewpie, which bore a striking resemblance to Cupid. When she progressed to drawing cut-out Kewpies for the *Woman's Home Companion*, toy makers began to take interest. The result was a world epidemic of bisque baby dolls. Kewpies were manufactured in their millions and snapped up with an alarming ferocity unparalleled until the arrival of Cabbage Patch Kids.

There were Kewpie towels, pin-hole cameras, magic lanterns, pillowcases, even Kewpie pipe-cleaners. In America Kewpies were, for a short time, one of the richest pickings of the consumer harvest. In Britain their big eyes and single tuft of hair made them a kind of national comforter, something to cling to in troubled times. Many Kewpies were made in Germany in the early days of World War I, and there was even a popular story that British Naval warships blockading the North Sea approaches turned a blind eye to a cargo ship, loaded with Kewpies, allowing it to offload in London.

There seemed nothing that Kewpies could not do. They wore military uniforms and dressed for the latest dance-craze, the Tango. In 1913, to a nation weaned on the

The 'Flying Colmars, Europe's Most Talented and Renowned Virtuoso Acrobatic Family'.

waltz, the Tango seemed sensuous, elegant and very exciting. Elsewhere, the zest for style sometimes ran out of control. Among the stage-door Johnnies who hung round the Gaiety Girls in a haze of cologne were the Knuts. These rich young loafers loved to parade in Piccadilly, preening themselves in dazzling socks, turn-up trousers and multi-coloured waistcoats. In the provinces, they were imitated by small armies of pimpled youths in cheap clothes. Recruiting sergeants appealing to the cream of Britain's manhood to join the Forces must have been reduced to apoplexy.

There was even a song about them:

> I'm Gilbert the Filbert, the Nut with a K
> The pride of Piccadilly, the blasé roué,
> Oh Hades, the ladies all leave their wooden huts
> For Gilbert the Filbert, the Colonel of the Knuts.

While conservative England looked hopefully for peace in the Kaiser's links with the Royal Family, the Knuts were busy bidding a last farewell to the old values. Even *The Times*, that upholder of everything sacred, could not overlook the importance of youth's last fling. Lord Northcliffe, the newspaper's owner, sent a celebrated memo to his editor in May 1913: '. . . One rigid rule I would make for the future is that on the personal page there should be nothing like "Scottish History Chair at Glasgow", which is of no interest to the distinguished Knuts and Flappers we are trying to pursue.' It was perhaps a final confirmation that the era had changed almost beyond recognition.

ON THE DANCE FLOOR, where etiquette and formality had set the pace since Victoria's day, there was almost wild abandon. A menagerie of animal dances arrived from America – the Bunny Hug, the Monkey Glide, the Buzzard Lope and the Turkey Trot:

> Everybody's doing it
> Doing what? The Turkey Trot!
> See that ragtime couple over there
> Watch them throw their shoulders in the air!

The older generation understandably found them outrageous and agreed wholeheartedly with the New Jersey judge who jailed one turkey-trotting girl for seven weeks for offending, well, just about everybody.

In England animal dances were all the rage among the young, but a degree of inhibition generally prevailed until Irene and Vernon Castle invented the Tango.

*Tango El Rococo* song-sheet.

This transatlantic partnership – Vernon was British, Irene American – was considered the most fashionable thing on four legs. Suddenly all the men were wearing wristwatches like Vernon (they had been a rarity up to 1913) and the girls all wanted their hair bobbed like Irene's.

In many ways it was a milestone. Daughters pleaded tearfully with their mothers until long Edwardian tresses covered the kitchen floors of Britain, and the last strands of the nineteenth century were swept away with them. Women were changing their looks in addition to moving away from the delicate, china-doll roles they had reluctantly played for so long. Street-sweeping skirts, popularized by Victoria, were replaced by hobble-skirts – tube-like creations which certainly lived up to their name, but accentuated the figure and announced a new independence. Fashion had to wait another decade for complete liberation when the flapper look celebrated women's increased confidence. The last word in hats was the *bonnet d'âne*, a velvet affair with donkey's ears sticking from the crown. The first brave girls to wear them tended, understandably, to walk around in groups, but wagging ears were soon seen all over London.

In those pre-war years, style was rapidly changing with a zest and optimism which appeared to accelerate as Britain neared the brink. Popular magazines, reaping the benefit of a literate working class, enjoyed booming circulations and fought cut-throat wars to win new readers. *John Bull*, *Answers* and *Titbits*, which was nicknamed the People's Times, laid the groundwork for modern tabloid journalism. While *John Bull* gave away spiralling sums in competition prizes, *Answers* offered a £1 a week for life to anyone who could guess the amount of gold in the Bank of England. The ever-political *Daily Express* contented itself with a major prize for the owner of the first parrot to say, 'Your food will cost you more.'

*Tea Time Tango* song-sheet.

*Titbits* was the innovator with the first football pools, and life insurance (valid only if the holder was found dead with a folded copy of *Titbits* in his pocket). Later an entire house was offered as a competition prize, something unheard of in those days. One of the conditions of the contest was that the winner had to call the house Titbits Villa for the rest of his life. When war broke out *Titbits* was the first to commission a song for the boys at the front. The writer, an unknown called Ivor Novello, dashed off *Keep The Home Fires Burning*. And no sooner had the guns cooled four years later than the enterprising *Titbits* leapt in again with an exclusive from the Kaiser: 'Why We Lost The War.'

Even *Boys' Own Paper*, started by Mrs Beeton's husband, Sam, bravely kept pace.

*Tit-Bits* advertisement (1910).

Old favourites such as 'Out with a jack-knife' by the Reverend J. G. Wood and 'Explosive spiders and how to make them' by Dr Scoffen, vanished under a rejigged format, pictures of space craft illustrating Jules Verne's serial *The Masters of the World* and diagrams of folding military bicycles. By *Boys' Own* standards it was a revolution.

Daily newspapers, too, had an ebullient cut-and-thrust in the days before accountants put a button on their rapiers, which made reading them almost as much fun as producing them. *Answers* – a venture blatantly stolen from *Titbits* by Alfred Harmsworth (later Lord Northcliffe), the self-styled Napoleon of Fleet Street – provided the capital to launch the *Daily Mail*. 'The busy man's newspaper' sold 800,000 copies a day to a solid middle-class readership. Those who disliked its stance accused it of being 'written by office boys for office boys.'

*The Daily Mirror*, the working man's tabloid, appeared in 1904 and instantly won a huge following with its easy-to-read layouts and expressive pictures. The art of newspaper photography owes much to the *Mirror*, but its early pioneers learned their skills the hard way. Photographer David McLellan, ordered to capture the magic of Piccadilly Circus by night, heaved himself onto the balcony of Swan and Edgar with his plate camera and tripod. No one ever discovered who mixed the magnesium powder so strongly, but the resulting explosion shattered fifty-two windows in surrounding buildings, and brought traffic to a halt.

The 1920s are properly associated with a taste for madcap diversions and mass crazes, but the years before World War I were equally deranged. Perhaps it was a universal urge to loosen collar studs and stays in the oppressive atmosphere before the approaching storm. There was talk of war for a long time before Regimental Sergeant Major Alhaji Grunshi of the Gold Coast Regiment fired the opening shot in 1914. For some, even that warning note seemed a long way from a peaceful England which, especially in country areas, was still slumbering in another age.

In the final months leading to the conflict, newspapers compiled a doleful catalogue of foreboding in Europe – wars in the Balkans, the assassination at Sarajevo, and then, with frightening rapidity, Germany and Austria were at war with Russia, France found itself drawn into the maelstrom, and, on Britain's doorstep, Belgium was invaded.

The inevitable drew nearer, but at home there were appetizing attractions to experience. A Mr Carter of London, for instance, had launched the first bags of potato crisps on an unsuspecting nation. Crisps had been a cottage industry in America for fifty years, and the idea had eventually found its way to France. Mr Carter tried them on holiday and was soon in full production.

One of his employees, Frank Smith, quickly left to set up a rival crisp factory, and had the whole of Britain rummaging in crackly bags for the small blue twist of salt, which was inevitably always at the bottom.

While life was never to be quite the same again after four gruelling years of war, people in 1913 were glimpsing a primitive, bewildering vision of the future. In the unhurried setting of Edwardian England, new ideas, soon to become commonplace, were greeted with enthusiastic curiosity. Victorians had had a thirst for novelties, gadgets and mechanical contraptions, but nothing to match the wonder that greeted gramophone records, wireless, refrigerators, Thermos flasks and cellophane. In the years before the outbreak of war news-

papers would gossip and crowds gather at the first hint of something new.

They blocked the pavements in London's Coventry street, stopping traffic to gaze at the words WEST END CINEMA glowing in the first spluttering display of neon. In Paris, where they took things more in their stride, there were more than a hundred neon signs on buildings. In London they brought an air of excitement and continental gaiety. It was appropriate that this most endemic of modern inventions hissed and flickered above a cinema. Old troupers of the theatre shrugged off the threat posed by silent, moving images, but the first trickle of talent was already deserting the music halls.

Thirty years earlier, music hall audiences had saluted the electric light which brought a jaundiced glow to the Crystal Palace:

*Boy's Own Paper* front page.

Oh, Mr Edison, whatever have you done?
Oh, Mr Edison, you've gone and spoilt our
    fun!
No more can we ramble with the girls all
    night;
The people, they will see us by the Electric
    Light.

Neon signs brought a new excitement, but no artist felt moved to sing the praises of the cinemas into which they were luring people in increasing numbers. By 1914, there were more than 3,500 hastily-converted picture houses across the country, licensed by 200 different companies.

Within ten years, a hundred London music halls had abandoned Variety, and the *Evening News* mourned their passing in a three-deck headline:

IS THE PUBLIC TASTE CHANGING?

THE CONQUERING FILM

PRE-WAR 'HOMELINESS' GONE FOR
    EVER

It summed up the swiftness of that first long stride into the twentieth century. One by one the halls – many with inspired architecture and beautiful interiors – were knocked down to make way for 'super-kinemas'. There was a grim irony, too, in the exodus of British variety artists to Berlin when the war ended. More music halls sprang up in the city than there had been in the whole of Germany a few years earlier.

THE CINEMA was not entirely to blame. Like many of today's businesses, managerial flair and enterprise had given way to the cold demands of accountancy. Variety had begun in bleak Northern towns and strutted to nationwide success, paying huge fees to star performers, and sowing the seeds of its own demise.

Albert Voyce, of the Variety Artists'

Federation blamed it on 'the power of men of purely financial interests and status.' He told the *Evening News*: 'The pre-war success of the music hall was due to the large number of men who studied the requirements and tastes of the cities and districts where they were placed, and very carefully selected the turns.

'With the coming of the financiers this special knowledge and personal selection has declined. New talent is not encouraged, since it seems easier to go on with the old stars than to foster new ones. . .'

Walter Payne, a director of thirty music halls, was struggling, along with many others, to compete with large fees paid to artists outside London. Small theatres were forced to close and, accelerated by the growth of the cinema, the tide of public taste was rapidly turning.

Live entertainment flourished in Edwardian times largely because of the great demand for diversions of any kind. It was the era when Jack Johnson was king of the boxing ring, and thousands cheered their home-grown hero Bombardier Wells, despite a chequered career of victories and defeats. In a small way British featherweight champion Ted 'Kid' Lewis made history, too, by slipping the first gumshield into his mouth.

Lancashire comedian Harry Weldon was quick to latch on to the immense popularity of boxing. When Australian heavyweight Colin Bell was knocked senseless in the second round by the Bombardier at Olympia, he slipped a line into his boxing sketch, 'The White Hope': 'Tell them what I did to Colin Bell (but don't tell them what he did to me). . .' At the East End's Wonderland and Premierland, and the arenas of Liverpool, Manchester and Birmingham, there was no shortage of contenders among the low paid and out-of-work eager to make money with their fists.

Buffalo Bill's Circus brought the Wild West to Britain with whooping Indians and rope-spinning cowboys. It was the heyday

National Sporting Club, December 1913. Carpentier swings a right to Wells' ribs.

of the travelling circus and the flamboyant Lord George Sanger's big top always drew the crowds.

'There is not, I believe, a town or village of over one hundred inhabitants in this United Kingdom I have not at some time or another visited,' his programme boasted. 'So, too, abroad. With the exception of Russia, I have carried my tents into every European country. . .'

The Sangers, who began as jesters in the court of King John, fought at the Battle of Trafalgar and were in the vanguard of performers who whipped up a growing mood of patriotism as war approached. Fifteen members of the family volunteered to fight as soon as war was declared. Ironically it was a shortage of petrol and animal feed in another world war which finally claimed the 120 year old family business.

Circus had glitter and spectacle on a grand scale, delivered to every town in Britain in the manner of travelling Variety. A world of wonder was little more than a tram ride away from most of the population. Comics and singers were Variety's stock-in-trade, but it could also produce epic thrills from its generous sleeve. There was, for instance, The Flood, a white-knuckle extravaganza which had audiences clenching their chairs as thousands of gallons of water rushed towards them and cascaded into a pool on-stage. A feat topped only by The Earthquake, with its tumbling plaster columns, deafening rumbles and flames roaring from hidden gas jets.

Even the 'legitimate' theatre was caught in the tidal wave of entertainment. George

Bernard Shaw was among those who complained that serious drama had been squeezed out by the Edwardian conception of a 'good night out'. Audiences watched Shakespeare mainly in order to see stars like Henry Irving and Beerbohn Tree performing amid lavish sets. Productions vied to outshine each other, a fashion which culminated in dozens of live rabbits hopping around under actors' feet in *Midsummer Night's Dream*.

They were memorable performances but one show, more than any other, left its impression on the age. *Hello Ragtime!* opened two nights before Christmas 1912 at the London Hippodrome, and within days half the city seemed to be humming its catchy, syncopated choruses. Rupert Brooke saw it ten times and was among thousands who packed the 451 sell-out performances to hear songs like:

> Come on and hear, come on and hear
>   Alexander's rag-time band,
> Come on and hear, come on and hear; it's
>   the best band in the land.
> They can play a bugle call like you never
>   heard before,
> So natural that you want to go to war.
> That's just the bestest band that am – honey
>   lamb,
> Come on along, come on along, let me
>   take you by the hand,
> Up to the man, up to the man who's the
>   leader of the band,
> And if you care to hear the Swanee River
>   played in rag-time,
> Come on and hear, come on and hear
>   Alexander's rag-time band.

Alexander's Ragtime Band by Irving Berlin © 1911 Irving Berlin Music Corp. USA sub-published B Feldman & Co Ltd.

Ethel Levey belted out the number flanked by a column of flag-waving drum majorettes. The show exploded with colour, energy and pizazz, introducing an unprepared Britain to the delights of American jazz. It was a welcome invasion which immediately captured the mood of the country.

Ragtime, alas, found few friends among

*Who's The Lady Now?* song-sheet.

those who wished to preserve the elegance and style which characterized the Edwardian era. 'If this is what they call music,' cried an incensed Lionel Monckton, who wrote the songs for the Gaiety musicals, 'then I write no more!' He was not alone – a few years later the carefree sounds which set the nation's feet tapping were to claim the life of Signor Nicola Coviello, director of the Balham School of Music. Signor Coviello, who had demonstrated his virtuosity on the cornet for both Queen Victoria and Edward VII, was visiting Coney Island when he encountered one of the dreaded jazz bands in the street. According to the *Daily Express*, in a report headed Musician Killed By Jazz: 'He was taking refreshment when a band close by suddenly blared. "This is not music!" said

*Alexander's Ragtime Band* song-sheet.

Signor Coviello, and putting his hands to his ears he fell to the pavement. Doctors said his death was due to heart strain.'

*Hello Ragtime!* was produced by Albert de Courville, a former journalist with an eye for what could capture the public imagination. His first enterprise had been to bring over from the Continent a boy called Meunier, and promote him as 'the Champion Diabolo Player of the World' on the music hall circuit. At the time the diabolo craze was in full swing, and there were inevitable challenges from the audience. De Courville, always the showman, arranged a mass diabolo play-off and, to his delight, thousands turned up. Police had to control the crowds, and many had to be turned away because the hall was not big enough. Unfortunately, every one of the

challengers proved to be vastly superior to his boy wonder.

*Hello Ragtime!* secured his reputation, though he had tried to bring jazz to Britain twelve months earlier by importing the American Ragtime Octet from Coney Island. The Hippodrome followed up its hit with *Hello Tango!* which gave impetus to yet another fad. For those of less frenzied persuasion, *The Passing Show* – staged almost on the eve of war – became the revue most poignantly associated with the passing of the era. It was a bright, witty, musical romp, with a young cast, billed as 'sparkling like champagne.' *The Passing Show*, often overlooked in the razamatazz of ragtime, leaves a sad picture of the young men in their silk evening scarves, puffing Abdullas, who patronized every performance. Many of them were to go to fight for their country, and never return.

PROGRESS was around for all to see, in the rattle of motor cars in the streets and the droning of frail machines criss-crossing the skies. By 1914, central London had dramatically changed. Kingsway and the Aldwych, with impressive buildings designed in an architectural competition, swept through a former maze of Dickensian alleyways. A few years earlier, with great foresight, Piccadilly had been cleared and widened to cope with increased traffic. More than 3,000 buses rattled on the city streets. Some were still horse-drawn, but the vast majority were now double-decker omnibuses with a staircase at the rear, and sides plastered with advertisements for Lipton's Tea and Wright's Coal Tar Soap. Handcarts were the most popular method of transporting goods for the poor, but they too were outnumbered by canvas-covered lorries trundling past the fast-disappearing horse and cart.

Britain's roads had not kept pace with the appearance of more than 132,000 cars by 1914, and drivers cursed the high streets pitted with pot holes. The horse had almost had its day – London's 5,000 horse-drawn hansom cabs were greatly outnumbered by honking black motor taxis. Even in the slower-paced countryside, tractors and traction engines were becoming a familiar sight, toiling over the patchwork fields.

In the absence of a highway code, road accidents were common. Frail cars, often with as little substance as a biscuit tin, came to grief in arguments with heavy trams, and could even be written off after colliding with a cart. As the ultimate badge of wealth and speed they were often driven with scant regard for safety. One alarmed historian, C. F. G. Masterman, recorded them as 'wandering machines racing with incredible velocity and no apparent aim' along country lanes and city streets.

In an epoch of contraptions the bicycle, too, was being manufactured in great numbers. The sight of ladies, pedalling furiously through busy thoroughfares, became an Edwardian novelty:

> My eye! Here's a lady bicyclist!
> Look at her! Look at her! Look at her! Look
>   at her!
> She's put her petticoats up the spout,
> And now she has to go without;
> She hopes her mother won't find out,
> And thinks they won't be missèd.
> Oh! My! Hi! Hi!
> Keep your eye on the lady bi-
> The lady bicyclist.

Beneath Londoners' feet lay the greatest wonder of them all, the Underground. Thousands poured up and down Tube station steps in the daily rush to work, despite the misgivings of a Parliamentary Committee which condemned the first

Dickensian alleyways were widened to cope with the increase in traffic.

proposals in 1891. 'The public,' it confidently predicted, 'will never consent to be squirted through a drain-pipe.' The public thoroughly enjoyed the Underground, braving the discomfort of choking air which swirled through tunnels and enveloped platforms in a sulphurous haze. So many people were using the Tube that a solution had to found to ease the twice-daily bottlenecks of humanity queuing for tickets.

As a result an escalator was unveiled at Earls Court Station in 1911. It was viewed with such apprehension that no more were constructed until after the war. Instructions were clearly posted for the nervous – 'passengers should alight with the left foot first' – and the *Illustrated London News* carried a double page spread explaining how it worked. There were, however, so many still fearful of putting their best foot forward, that London Transport was obliged to pay a man with a wooden leg to ride up and down all day, thus demonstrating that anyone could do it.

Above ground, in the bustling widened streets, one of the more immediate changes Londoners noticed was the noise. Only ten years earlier the decibel level of a city was little more than that of a county town, punctuated with cries of street-vendors and the clatter of horse-drawn carriages. In the last whole year of peace before the war, window panes rattled to the rumble of the Underground, and the air was filled with the sound of revving engines.

Petrol and steam provided speed and excitement. Edwardians, always keen for new experiences, could not bear to see anything so exhilarating harnessed merely to everyday transport. Mechanical ingenuity found expression in the fairground, with breathtaking rides which capitalized on the nationwide need for adrenalin.

Blaring Orchestraphones with 110 keys and the power of a crazed orchestra, strings of electric lights and brilliant carbon arc lamps turned fairgrounds into a riot of

Fairgrounds became a riot of noise and colour.

noise and colour. Bioscopes showing jerky two-reelers were invariably the centrepiece of each site – huge primitive touring cinemas, with 12 m (40 ft) frontages elaborately carved and painted, and a steam organ to pull in the crowds. With advances in engineering, rides like 'the gallopers' could travel at remarkable speeds. As the war years approached they began to greatly outnumber the old side-show attractions. Showmen remember 1912 and 1913 as the most lucrative years that travelling fairs have known.

One proprietor, offering his razzle-dazzle ride for sale, claimed in his advertisement that it earned him £150 a day. It was small wonder that serious entertainments, such as the Gilbert and Neilsen Opera Company, were forced into liquidation. The manager, explaining his predicament to the London Bankruptcy Court, confessed that the public 'preferred cake-walks and coon songs to classical music'. Nancy, Susie and the Three Gentlemen sang about one of London's favourite background attractions:

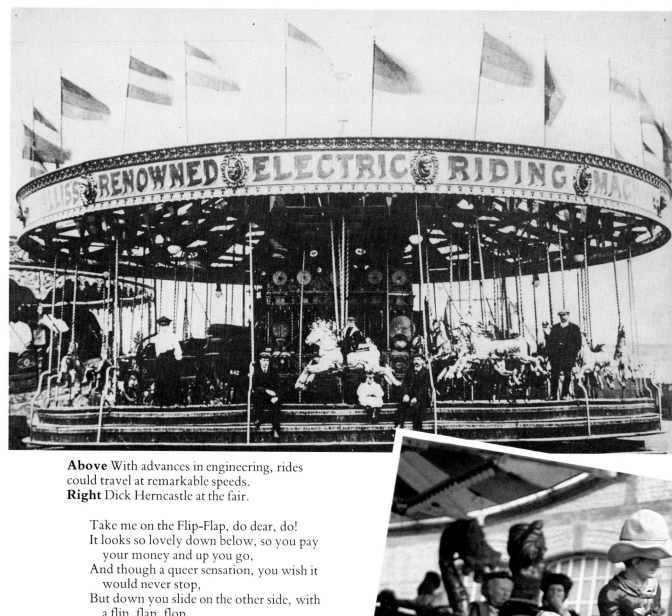

**Above** With advances in engineering, rides could travel at remarkable speeds.
**Right** Dick Herncastle at the fair.

> Take me on the Flip-Flap, do dear, do!
> It looks so lovely down below, so you pay
>     your money and up you go,
> And though a queer sensation, you wish it
>     would never stop,
> But down you slide on the other side, with
>     a flip, flap, flop.

Higher still, aircraft were becoming a familiar sight over towns and villages. Amazingly, no one had given much thought to their economic potential, and only a few realized their military significance. There was, however, a flurry of interest in aviation when the *Daily Mail*, with great foresight, offered a £10,000 prize for the first successful flight between London and Manchester. By 1911, mail flights were run experimentally between Hendon and Windsor, but passenger flight was almost unheard of. Germany, on the other hand, had carried 35,000 passengers by Zeppelin by 1914, but both sides shelved the development of domestic flights until after 1918.

Aircraft were put to military use within days of war breaking out. The first two British aviators to be killed in action lost their lives in August 1914, when their lumbering Henri Farman, weighed down with a heavy machine gun, was strafed by a German Albatross. Only six months into the war the enemy launched its first bombing raid on England. Terror from the skies became a new fear for a public who had hailed the wonder of flight, only to find it turned against them. Fortunately, the bomb, dropped from 1524 m (5,000 ft), only blew a hole in the lawn of St James' Rectory, Dover, and broke the incumbent's windows. Bomb fragments were later dug from the flower bed and mounted on a commemorative shield which was presented to King George v.

D ESPITE THE misfortunes of the Gilbert and Neilsen Opera Company, the pre-war years were rich in art, music and literature – possibly the last great liberal period in English history, according to some historians. It was the age of Shaw, Havelock Ellis, Galsworthy and H. G. Wells. D. H. Lawrence wrote his earthy masterpiece *Sons and Lovers* in 1913 and, a year later, Joyce's *Dubliners* appeared. Even popular fiction experienced new delights with Chesterton's Father Brown stories, Edgar Wallace and, imported from America, Edgar Rice Burrough's tales of Tarzan. On the music front, Holst, Elgar, Vaughan Williams and Delius were in their prime. And while newspapers chattered about the theft and recovery of the Mona Lisa from the Louvre, Picasso, Mondrian and Chagall were quietly at work changing the art world. Percy Wyndham Lewis was busily launching Vorticism, a hybrid of Futurism and Cubism which, though short-lived, reflected the violent labour pains of the

twentieth century. 'All beauty is based on strife,' their manifesto declared as the golden age slid dangerously nearer to war.

Most ordinary people were unaware of the significant influences emerging from the arts. Life for the upper classes had a certain solid satisfaction, while the mainstream of the population was lost in a vorticism of its own. Those with money to spend could dispose of it in chains of department stores. As manufacturing became geared to mass markets it was inevitable that shopping should undergo a similar revolution. Gordon Selfridge opened a department store in Oxford Street with 1,800 staff; and goods were illuminated in the windows at night. When Blériot flew the Channel, Selfridge immediately negotiated to put his wood and canvas flying machine on show to draw in the crowds. Waring and Gillow and other large shops began to change the Oxford Street skyline. Despite cramped housing and people sleeping rough, Londoners had money to spend and, for the first time, were faced with a dazzling choice of ways to spend it.

In the last years of peace, city life was as good as a free show unless you happened to be poor, and then the brave new world made little difference. Vast fortunes made during the rise of Victorian industry had done little – apart from the efforts of a few paternal factory owners – to improve the lot of a huge section of the common people. The great pyramid of privilege was firmly cemented by the class system. Life at the top was carefree, and cushioned with a comfortable sense of continuity. The rich found it reassuring that their sons would inherit their titles or take over the tiller of the family business. The poor, at the bottom, found little to lighten their plight. Unemployment benefit at 7s (35p) a week, maternity benefit at 30s (£1·50), and 10s (50p) a week sickness payment for those in work were introduced early in 1913 to ease social problems.

Selfridges in March 1909.

Deep divisions in society made it clear that hardship was the lot of the majority – perhaps not imposed by God as Victorians were fond of suggesting, but unavoidable all the same. But even if hardship seemed unavoidable, there was a noticeable drop in demand for the music hall songs of a few years earlier which promoted the notion. Had he been around in 1913, Harry Clifton, the 'Hoddesden drawing room vocalist', would have encountered thin applause for numbers like *Work, Boys, Work and be Contented, Up with the Lark in the Morning*, and *Put your Shoulder to the Wheel is a Motto for Every Man*.

Then try to be happy and gay, boys,
Remember the world is wide
And Rome wasn't built in a day, boys,
So wait for the turn of the tide.

Everyone had heard of Archduke Franz-Ferdinand, and a few of Sarajevo in a faraway place called Bosnia. But, perhaps because the gleaming red open tourer and cheering crowds lining the cobbled streets seemed set in some distant comic-opera, no one was prepared for the unexpected swiftness of the events which followed. It was as though an unseen hand was frantically mixing the ingredients of war.

The single shot that shook the world took only a fraction of a second. Gavrilo Princip, a teenage member of a team of seven gunmen planted at intervals along the route by the Serbian nationalist Black Hand Gang, stepped forward and fired at Franz-Ferdinand with a heavy revolver, hitting him in the neck. The bullet was deflected by a bone and ricochetted, killing the Duchess Sophie sitting beside him.

The poor, at the bottom, found little to lighten their plight.

Ironically, Ferdinand's love of pomp and Ruritanian pageant contributed to his death. His heavily-braided tunic, festooned with medals, was so tightly buttoned that officers who tore at it desperately could not open it, and he bled to death. His car, which stood forgotten in the confusion, became one of those oddities which often accompany turning points of history – its number plate, A111-118, proved somewhat remarkably to forecast the date of Armistice Day, on 11 November, 1918.

The enormity of the assassination which plunged England into war had an unreal quality. Newsboys shouted the Archduke's death from street corners, but little could shake ordinary people from the belief that war was unthinkable. The drama remained distant until it was all too late. Many of the accounts of how people heard the news in an England which still had one foot in the nineteenth century, suggest that the speed of events took time to sink in. For most of them it was little more than a solitary cloud in an azure sky.

Journalist Hoole Jackson recalled: 'As I cycled home from the Lake District to Manchester one lovely afternoon, the red admirals and small copper butterflies danced with others in the air above the wayside flowers. I took my ease along the quiet, dusty main road, taking a flagon at a wayside inn, along with thick, rich slices of ham. There seemed nothing to break the comfortable dream of the future.

'The newsboys were shouting as I rode into the city. I bought a paper and read that Archduke Ferdinand had been assassinated. Sarajevo was a long way off. These foreigners were always trying to murder some-

lovely morning in June 1914, I motored into Tisbury. As the tank was being filled, I idly noted a poster which said "Murder of an Austrian Archduke." There was an exquisite summer haze enveloping the soft, contented South Wiltshire landscape, and Austria and murdered Archdukes seemed foreign, foolish and far away. . .'

Within a few short months the lost summer became the final memory of a passing age, before the cruel machinery of war claimed twenty million lives throughout Europe. Shortly before her death in Monte Carlo in 1952, Vesta Tilley looked back: 'We knew that we had seen the end of an era,' she recalled. 'Those wonderful Edwardian years were the best of all. Even though we may be able to fly to America between breakfast and lunch, or hop to the Moon for the weekend, life will never be quite the same again. . .'

Newsboys proclaim: DEATH AT SARAJEVO.

VARIETY, like newspapers at the time, had little affection for foreigners and lampooned them at every opportunity. There were few variety bills which did not feature performers from all over Europe and America and, while backstage there was no prejudice, comedians found the tradition of English superiority a reliable stand-by for cheap laughs. The first indications of impending war were quickly seized by artists with a keen nose for current affairs. Audiences were soon swaying to patriotic songs and chuckling at the numerous jokes about the Kaiser.

Some of the numbers had been hastily dusted-down from the Russian-Turkish war, but they went down well, and no one was complaining.

one. There had been talk in my boyhood about Ferdinand – was it in 1900? I recalled my elders talking about him. Why all the newspaper hullaballoo?

'At home the bank manager poohpoohed the idea of war. Germany would be ruined within three months financially if she were fool enough to go to war. Couldn't last. He produced facts and figures most convincingly. Then the tiny avalanche began to grow; nation after nation became involved. Belgium was invaded and the British ultimatum to Germany ran out – the impossible had happened. . .'

Desmond Huston recorded similar feelings in *The Lamp of Memory*: 'Early on a

> We don't want to fight
> But, by jingo, if we do,
> We've got the men
> We've got the ships
> We've got the money too. . .

Soldiers on show in the streets.

G. H. Macdermott first sang his song at the London Pavilion in 1878, coining a new word – jingoism – in the English language. His other numbers, *Dear Old Pals* and *True Blues Stand By Your Guns*, never achieved quite the public impact as the song he bought for a guinea from Henry Pettitt.

A few weeks after the first performance William Minto, the great *Daily News* leader writer used 'jingo' to refer to vocal patriotism. Two days later a letter landed on Minto's desk from George Jacob Holyoake, a well-known agitator, which ranted about 'the Jingoes, the new tribe of music hall patriots who sing the Jingo Song.' But, sensing its wide appeal, Holyoake could not resist jumping on the bandwagon, and claimed: 'I am, if you like, a Jingo, a word which, by the way, I was the first person ever to write – at the dictation of my late uncle George Jacob Holyoake.' He was wrong, of course. 'Hey jingo!' was first used by conjurors as the equivalent of 'Hey presto!' In 1700 there was even a popular game called 'Hey

jinko!', 'in great request among our merry sailors in Wapping.'

But whatever its origin, the song of the Great Macdermott, as he billed himself, rekindled the flame of patriotism among variety audiences. All the preaching of powerful newspapers and pontificating politicians could do little to match the immediacy of Variety. While the former shouted slogans, it was the chummy chaps in crumpled check suits and the down-to-earth girls beyond the footlights that the great mass of people actually dug into their pockets to see. The roaming band of variety artists who shared their problems, sang about their hopes and fears and summed up life with a wink and a nudge, were understood in the vast land of tin baths and back-to-backs north of Luton.

Tragedy and comedy have a habit of going hand in hand, and the belly laughter which rocked those hollow auditoriums as war approached had an unsettling ring. 'It wasn't innocent and natural, as the soft laughter between friends could be,' says

Dick Herncastle. 'There was something fierce and vindictive about it, not coming from happy people but from those whose bewilderment deepening to despair was not a mask. I noticed, as we played in so many different towns, that the poorer and darker the streets surrounding us, the closer we were to misery, the louder and harder the laughter was.'

A powerful, almost frightening, flame of patriotism lit up the country. Variety theatres glowed like Edwardian versions of the hill-top beacons which had announced the Armada centuries earlier. 'Words and

Variety theatres, like the rest of the country, glowed with a powerful flame of patriotism.

melodies pass by quick magic from the Empire to the Alhambra over the length and breadth of the land, re-echoed in a thousand provincial halls, clubs and drinking saloons, until the remotest village is familiar with the air and sentiment. . .'

It had a long tradition – Harry Gordon, with his kilt and crofter's crook, had made a fortune from patriotic sketches such as *On Guard – A story of Balaclava*. Surrounding himself with flags, and a series of quick costume changes from Drake to General Gordon, he had a rousing song for most of the major battles of British history. The audience stamped their feet in marching time until the rococo plasterwork threatened to crash down on them.

> Oh, fighting with the 7th Royal Fusiliers!
> Famous Fusiliers, gallant Fusiliers.
> Through deadly Russian shot and Cossack
>     spears,
> We carved our way to glory. . .'

A stopwatch operation took Gordon by hansom cab to three different theatres a night, earning him £5000 a year while the sun shone on the British Empire.

With the outbreak of war, stars were provided with another opportunity to carve their way to glory. While many genuinely supported the war effort, there was no doubt that the mood of the times helped to sustain their popularity in the days when Music Hall was fading. Others found to their cost that war fever had an adverse effect. A wave of anti-German feeling swept the country, and in the streets around the great variety theatres, shops with German-sounding names had their windows smashed and stock looted. Working turns who had settled in England from Europe felt uneasy as mobs rampaged looking for obvious targets.

One of the tragic casualties was Paul Cinquevalli, a superb juggler who had appeared at the Royal Command Performance in 1912. Rumour spread that he was

The conscription drive reaches the variety stage.

German and his career was marred by threats and hysteria until, completely dejected, he was forced into retirement in 1915. It was a sign of the remarkable fervour of nationalism whipped up at the time that the public could turn on talented performers who, only months before, they had cheered and idolized. Cinquevalli was in fact Polish, but had been educated in Berlin. He settled in London and perfected tricks which have seldom been equalled. One of them, The Human Billiard Table, involved playing billiards on his own back with great precision. His act invariably ended with the trick everyone wanted to see – throwing a heavy iron cannonball high in the air, and catching it on the back of his neck.

If Cinquevalli was broken by the war, others thrived on it. Harry Champion entertained the first troops home on leave at park concerts with quick-fire songs such as *Any Old Iron* and *I'm Henry The Eighth I Am*. After weeks on iron rations in the trenches there were wild cheers for his amazing repertoire of songs about food that would have made a vegetarian wince – *Boiled Beef And Carrots*, *Boiled Sheep's Hearts*, *I Like Pickled Onions*, *Hot Tripe And Onions*, *Hot Meat Pies*, *Saveloys And Trotters*. . . Harry summed up everything they had been dreaming about.

Vesta Tilley threw herself so wholeheartedly into the conscription drive that she became known as 'England's finest recruiting sergeant.' After cheering songs with such dubious titles as *We Don't Want To Lose You*, hundreds of young men would leave their seats to sign army papers offered by waiting sergeants:

Vesta Tilley in
uniform.

We've watched you playing cricket and
    every kind of game,
At football, golf and polo you men have
    made your name.
But now your country calls you to play
    your part in war.
And no matter what befalls you
We shall love you all the more.
So come and join the forces
As your fathers did before.
Oh, we don't want to lose you but we
    think you ought to go.
For your King and your country both need
    you so.
We shall want and we shall miss you
But with all our might and main
We shall cheer you, thank you, bless you
When you come home again.

The shaken, disorientated boys who did
come home were greeted by music hall and
variety stars who sang to the wounded in
military hospitals. Marie Lloyd gave much
of her time to this. Ada Reeve, another
popular musical comedy star, was among
artists who embarked on a crusade to
entertain troops both at home and behind
the lines. As a result her song, *The Long,
Long Trail*, became one of the most
requested of the war years. Like many of
its type it was cloyingly sentimental; and
this added to the hint of the fear, foremost
in everyone's mind, that the troop trains
leaving Victoria Station were often a one-
way ride.

There's a long, long trail a-winding
Into the land of my dreams
Where the nightingales are singing
And the white moon beams
There's a long, long night of waiting,
Until my dreams come true
On the day when I'll be going down
That long, long trail with you.

It expressed perfectly the hopes of those at home who could do little more than sit it out and wait for peace. In the blasted landscape of Flanders, the soldiers were more forthright in their own ballads, which drifted from beneath corrugated tin sheets pounded by perpetual rain:

I want to go home
I want to go home
I don't want to go to the trenches no more,
Where the guns and whiz-bangs and
    cannons do roar,
I want to go home
Where the Germans they can't get at me,
Oh my, I don't want to die,
I want to go home.

*Jack and Tommy's favourite patriotic tunes.*

NONETHELESS, back home the patriotic mood pervaded both sides of the footlights. Comedians Morris and Cowley, then billed as the Birkenhead Family, were among the first to enlist, along with a brother who was in the act with them. While some artists were to lose their lives in action, others distinguished themselves on the battlefield. Bunny Doyle, a Hull comedian, was among the first wave of recruits to sail for France. He found himself in great demand from the West Yorkshire Regiment concert party, and was also awarded the Croix de Guerre for gallantry. Billy Bennett, one of Variety's most famous names who made a trademark of his walrus moustache and hobnail boots, won both the Croix de Guerre and the Distinguished Conduct Medal, but never referred to them on his return to civilian life.

The war threw Variety, along with the rest of the country, into confusion. Managers struggled to cobble bills together as artists joined the rush to enlist. Those abroad on tour found themselves caught by the turmoil sweeping through Europe. Harry Lauder was playing to packed houses in Melbourne, with songs like *Roamin' In The Gloamin'* and *I Love A Lassie*, when war was declared. The cast hurriedly met to discuss whether to return home, but finally took the advice of another of Harry's songs, *Keep Right On To The End Of The Road*, and pressed on to New Zealand and America.

Variety stars urged their audiences to

Harry Lauder.

sign up and fight, and when the packed troop trains toiled across northern France to the front, their songs were remembered, lifting moral and, as the weeks went by, making at least a few aware of the absurdity of the 'war to end wars'. Fred Karno's slapstick routines had given rise to the expression Fred Karno's Army, which the muddy, bedraggled infantrymen lost no time turning into song:

> We are Fred Karno's Army
> A jolly lot are we
> Fred Karno is our captain
> Charles Chaplin our O.C.
> And when we get to Berlin
> The Kaiser he will say
> *Hoch, Hoch, Mein Gott*
> What a jolly fine lot
> Are the boys of Company A.

When the survivors finally marched home there was no gleam of victory in their eyes, only the crushed expression of young men who had seen too much before their time. Many of them parodied the words of one of the most popular love songs of the era – Jerome Kern's *They Didn't Believe Me* – which, after long months enduring the horrors of battle, had taken on a bitter new meaning.

> And when they asked us how dangerous it
>     was.
> Oh! We'll never tell them,
> No, we'll never tell them.
> We spent our pay in some café,
> And fought wild women night and day,
> T'was the cushiest job we ever had.
>
> And when they ask us, and they're
>     certainly going to ask us.
> The reason why we didn't win the Croix
>     de Guerre.
> Oh! We'll never tell them,
> No, we'll never tell them.
> There was a front but damned if we knew
>     where.

# WORKING TURNS

Trains cross, carrying variety artists from show to show.

THE ONLY fare-paying passengers waiting on the platform of Crewe station on a Sunday, so the saying goes, were actors and fish. The fish, of course, were dead – stacked in boxes waiting for delivery to the Monday morning markets of Britain. The actors, usually variety artists moving on to the next town after a week's run, were almost in the same condition. Crewe station, rising like a soot-stained cast-iron cathedral, seemed to have the coldest platforms in the country. Winds howled through the open-ended train hall, forcing chorus girls into huddles on parcel trollies. Groups of them waved to friends on the opposite platform, waiting for trains to other parts of the country. Each Sunday brought a similar scene: the working turns gathered in the middle of the platform, exchanging gossip; while a suitable distance apart, the top of the bill wrapped in cashmere, sat alone on his trunk, maintaining even in transit the aura of stardom. Crewe became the Variety Artists' Sunday Club – an opportunity to renew old friendships, pass on letters and warn of digs to be avoided.

The platforms were stacked with wicker hampers packed with costumes and long poles, around which were rolled painted back-cloths and scenery. Big name performers with elaborate acts had their own rail vans, while working turns made the best of the guard's van stacking their props among the mail bags, fish boxes and pigeon baskets. They often had to purchase their own canvas backdrop and haul it, like a terrible millstone, throughout their working lives.

Many had a working plan of the railways engraved in their mind, and could recite train times and connections with the authority of Bradshaw. Crucial to this knowledge were the great 'intermediate' stations and their buffets – Crewe and Rugby where passengers were allowed a twenty minute stop for food; Preston where half a meal could be snatched before changing for Scotland. At Wolverton there was a stampede for the refreshment room when the train stopped for ten minutes. 'Seven very young ladies' dispensed pork pies and banbury cakes with a choice of seven kinds of drink from rum to stout, but not including whisky. At York the pace was more leisurely – a thirty minute refreshment stop was included in the time table.

Dining halts were the signal for intense activity on the platform, presided over by the station master in his top hat and frock coat, enhanced occasionally with white gloves and a red carnation. At Crewe there was almost a theatrical touch as he paced like a master of ceremonies, framed by the grey proscenium arch of the signal gantry at the end of the platform. South Western platform staff scuttled around in red ties which they had to cut out and sew themselves from a six-monthly issue of company twill. In emergencies, 'when no red flag is available', they were expected to whip off their neckwear and wave them as a danger signal. (This admirably practical idea survived until 1926 when the board of directors decided that blue ties clashed less with the colour-scheme of the uniform.)

One of the biggest attractions for artists waiting in the buffet was piping hot soup – carriage heating was in its infancy before World War I – and even in those days travellers complained about the food. The

Dick Herncastle and Barney running for a train.

soup was invariably so hot that the departure bell would ring long before it was cool enough to taste, and the rush to board the train began. One weary passenger, complaining about the refreshment room salad, likened it to 'eating a gravel walk and coming across the occasional weed.' Wolverton's pork pies were legendary – in the ten minutes allowed to eat them one passenger consumed a dozen and then complained to the buffet manager that no one could be expected to live on fare like that.

On trains travelling west to Bristol's new Hippodrome, with its saucer ceiling designed to slide open on summer nights, the outlook was brighter. Arrangements could be made for the guard to telegraph ahead for a lunch basket to be waiting at the next station. When the first restaurant cars were introduced stars were spared the undignified mêlée round the refreshment room, but the standard of food did not improve. Meals prepared in the early swaying coal-fired kitchens had so much

grit in them that gas cylinders had to be introduced to improve the standard of cooking.

Passengers found the prospect of taking a drink back to their compartment such a novelty that Great Western Railway staff found themselves sweeping up 130 broken glasses a week. Before the system improved, drinks had to be ordered in the dining car where the attendant would pass the list to a boy who had to dash into the buffet at the next station. Theatricals were clearly in need of great fortification, because the list was often so long that he would miss the train, and the order would have to be repeated at the next stop.

The Midland, the Great Northern, the North-Western and Great Western all served 'soup, fish and joint' in sumptious surroundings, and bill-toppers travelling first class began to feel at last that they were being treated in a manner in which they would like to become accustomed.

'The car is sixty feet long with a body of oak, panellings of Honduras mahogany, and finishings in American walnut, while the ceilings are richly painted and decorated', one travel writer enthused. 'A dozen seats, richly upholstered in crimson morocco are placed transversely on either side of the central passage. This arrangement gives a separate seat for each traveller, while between each couple of seats a moveable table can be fixed and electric bells at hand enable passengers to summon the attendants at any time.

'The whole appearance is that of a handsome and luxurious saloon, while the seats tend to prevent the motion of the train being felt.' There was also the attractive advantage that each monstrous dining car weighed 33 tons and was usually the only carriage to survive a crash intact.

The rest of the cast would invariably travel third class where comfort and heating were less in evidence. By the war, however, improvements in rail travel had made the problems of getting around the country less of an ordeal.

Life between performances was a drab, timeless existence, spent whiling away empty days in obscure towns, waiting for the warmth and applause of the evening performance. Away from the footlights, strangely pallid in the daylight without greasepaint, they moved like strangers in a strange land. Priestley has Ricarlo, the Italian juggler in *Lost Empires*, 'moving week after week, month after month, from one Empire to the next, through a succession of gloomy and alien industrial towns . . . like places in a bad dream.'

At the end of the journey, in Oldham, Bradford or Hull, the whole process of

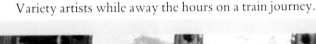

Variety artists while away the hours on a train journey.

unloading the props would begin again, counting them out from the guards van into horse-drawn pantechnicons waiting to deliver them to the theatre. Even with the greatest care the unexpected mishap could always happen. Chorus girl Millicent Montague faced the unwelcome prospect of having to wear wet costumes because stage-hands had left the property hampers out in the rain.

'The chorus found that their dresses were soaking wet, not just damp, but really wet,' she recalled. 'We refused to put the clothes on, and the distracted dresser ran for the stage manager to tell him "the girls have struck". That brought him hurrying, and full of expostulations. The pit and the gallery were getting restive when he dashed out, returning hastily with numerous bottles of whisky, of which he made each of us drink down half a tumbler "to keep off the chill". Fortified by this, and with his promise that the dresses should be dried before the next performance, we went on, but more than one bronchial cold and "go" of 'flu was traceable to that night's work.'

Even artists fortunate enough to live near the theatre they happened to be playing encountered transport problems. In the early 1900s Espinosa, who led a dancing troupe, found himself booked at Shepherd's Bush Empire as the final act on the bill. Shows often ran until midnight, when public transport had stopped, so in desperation he begged his manager to telegram the formidable theatre owner Oswald Stoll to ask if he could go on earlier. Off went the message: 'Will you kindly alter my time. I am last act on and live eighteen miles from the theatre. How can I do it?' And by return came the legendary reply: 'Move' – Stoll.

Digs were a recurring nightmare, and artists guarded the priceless address books like state secrets. Warm, cheap accommodation with good food was a prize to treasure, and one which was often acquired

Landladies – the butt of countless variety jokes.

by bitter experience. The comedian's only weapon against grasping landladies was to turn them into the butt of countless variety jokes: 'I say, missus. There's a kipper in the mousetrap under my bed.' Landlady: 'Well, I warned you it was a damp room.'

Theatrical dwarves in particular led a miserable existence, sometimes receiving callous treatment from landladies who resented them occupying a full-size bed. More than one had to suffer the indignity of sleeping in a vegetable box at the foot of another artist's bed.

The smell of stale cooking, a coal fire struggling for survival and a faded print of the Monarch of the Glen were enough to make the heart of the most seasoned tourer sink. Many recall that the worst landladies had a habit of stressing how wonderful their accommodation was, with its 'new pelvises on the curtains, seduced lighting and the lovely muriel in the parlour.' This endless chatter could grate on the frayed nerves of performers. 'How would you like your eggs, dear?' one fussing hostess is said to have asked Bransby Williams, famed for his histrionic readings from Shakespeare. 'In silence, madam!' Bransby boomed. Sir Bernard Miles recalls a granite-faced Northern landlady showing him to a spartan room and warning: 'Guests are requested not to replace the chamber-pot under the bed after use, as the steam rusts the springs.' This is, perhaps, frank enough to render anyone speechless.

'Since the bitter experiences of my first tour, the top third of my wicker hamper is always filled with my own eiderdown,' one variety girl of 1913 recalled after shivering under muslin blankets. 'The other girls laugh at me when they first see it, but later, when they are having to go on with the racking headaches that accompany heavy colds, and their streaming eyes and noses force them to make-up afresh between every act, it is my turn to laugh – only I can't, because it would be too unkind. For economy's sake chorus girls generally share a double bed, and I often wonder if is is my eiderdown that makes me so much in request among my friends.'

There were, too, landladies with hearts of gold who would sit up all night applying hot poultices to acrobats' strained muscles rather than see them lose their pay. One Manchester landlady even redecorated the bedroom of a star who was superstitious about green. A few had been working turns themselves and understood their guests' inverted lifestyles of late rising and midnight dinners.

Vera Blades of Davyhulme, Manchester, grew up in theatrical digs run by her mother who made her stage debut in 1910, singing with her friend Daisy Cowen in a duo called the Blends. They travelled as curtain-raisers for stars such as Harry Lauder, George Formby Snr. and Will Hays' father.

'The lights, the money, the audience and the way it all reacts on you was a tremendous thing to her,' Mrs Blades recalls. 'As far as she was concerned, that was the life. They were never at the bottom of the bill, or the splash across the bill, they were just filling in. Their songs were the popular songs of the day. They would finish on Saturday night, pack their stage trunks and baskets and get everything ready for moving off on Sunday.

'They had to have their own hand-written band parts, and carried their own back-cloths. It was a very busy life involving a lot of tedious travel. There was sometimes friction backstage. I can remember mother saying they'd words with the manager, and that they would never go back to that theatre again, or they would complain that conditions were not good enough. I suppose it was good pay – they were earning in the region of ten pounds a week in those days. If you disagreed with something, you still had to do it because it was your bread and butter.

'In those days it was just as common to get your contract by sleeping around as it is now. It was known as "via Richard", but I have never heard that from anyone except my mother. The theatre managers would ensure that you got your booking and that a good report went to your agent, processed "via Richard", which we all thought was highly entertaining.'

Eventually, after Mrs Blades' mother had her dress chewed by a goat on stage, and Daisy Cowen narrowly missed being decapitated by a falling fly, the act broke up and she opened a boarding house for fellow curtain-raisers. 'We didn't have top quality people,' says Mrs Blades, 'No one famous. They would have a bedroom and come down for their meal, or use the best room at the front. It was hard work because you had to move like the artists – changing the beds, cleaning the rooms and the house as soon as they moved out on Sunday morning, ready for the next intake on Sunday night. They had to pay their lodgings straight away before they left. It was always in cash. Cheques didn't exist for them.'

On Sunday mornings, often when performers were still sleeping, the theatre property men would make a tour of the digs, collecting hampers in horse-drawn

Dick and Nancy take a ride in a gig.

carts to take to the station. The going rate was 1s 6d (7½p), but not everyone took up the offer. Some struggling artists preferred to carry their own to save money and, if they happened to be among those who used a horse or donkey as part of the act, the animals would be pressed into service to shoulder the luggage.

IT TOOK A certain iron determination to work with an animal stooge, and not everyone could summon it, or indeed, find the stamina to sustain it. Burlesque comedian Robert Hale, who specialized in impersonations of famous people and well-known trades, appeared in one sketch as a bargee, accompanied by a horse.

'The animal – a piebald of some sixteen hands – had been trained in a special way,' he recalled. 'When his rider pressed a certain brown spot, the horse performed a certain action – stood on his hind legs, nodded his head, and so on. Well, I spent hours trying to learn which spot meant action and, so long as the trainer was with me, I was able to put the piebald through his paces. There was very little time left, so I was only able to have a few rehearsals.

'On the opening night I was a mass of nerves, and the horse gave me an unpleasant glance when I mounted and trotted him to the stage. With a trembling hand I pressed the spot which meant "kneel down". Evidently it was the wrong one, for nothing happened. I thought hard and pressed another – wrong again! This annoyed the horse, and when I pressed yet one more he bucked me off. In despair I reached up and tapped a spot – and the brute opened his mouth and ran at me. An exciting chase ensued, and I dashed off the stage, followed by the furious animal. The audience rolled with laughter, thinking it was intentional; but I refused to give an encore.'

Animals could be relied upon to play a leading role in any great theatrical disaster, but stage-hands occasionally came a close second. Comedienne Ada Reeve appeared in a provincial Edwardian pantomime which called for her to leap from a precipice into her lover's arms. On the first night, in the middle of the scene, she found that no means of climbing up to the precipice had been provided.

*Ideas Magazine* was there to capture the

Edwardians, hungry for novelty, loved any kind of animal act.

moment: 'A number of dress baskets were hastily dragged onto the stage and piled one on top of the other,' it reported. 'Upon these Miss R mounted. The time arrived for the hero to exclaim, "Where, oh! where art thou, my love?" and for her to reply, "I am here." But just as this touching incident was about to be enacted, the pile of baskets began to slip and, instead of jumping into her lover's arms, Miss R fell over the precipice and landed on his shoulders. For a moment or two he succeeded in supporting her, and then he and she ignominiously collapsed onto the stage amid the shouts of the audience.'

Edwardians, hungry for novelty, loved any kind of animal act, from Duncan's Collies to Woodward's Seals. A chimp of superior intelligence – superior to some of his audiences, anyway – was a great attraction on the Northern variety circuits. At Wakefield, Consul was examined by twenty medical students before going on stage at the Hippodrome. The highlight of his act was to recline in an armchair and ring a bell to summon a butler with a tray of bananas. Consul's antics were a delight, more so perhaps because they unconsciously aped the languid image of the upper classes.

In 1907, there was great pressure to make Lockhart's Elephants – Vinegar, Spicey,

Salt and Mustard – join the variety artists' strike. Mr Lockhart explained to leaders of the dispute that he had tried to ballot the animals, but had been unable to discover their views. As a result the elephants were in great demand, lumbering between theatres for two, even three, performances a day. There is no record of anyone attempting to stop them crossing the picket line.

The dispute, over working conditions, was led by the newly-formed Variety

Impressario Chance Newton was called in to arbitrate in the Music Hall War, as it was quickly called: 'Things began to rule very lively. The Tivoli, the Pavilion, the Oxford and other important Variety theatres were struck against. In fact all manner of variety houses and music halls were "proclaimed", so to speak, and were picketed by artistes and variety stage folk of all kinds. These insurgents were led by the leading stars, who orated at meetings, not only within doors, but also out in the

'The Duffield Dogs Presenting Canine Capers and Amazing Antics from the Foremost Animal Act in the Land.'

Artists' Federation, and backed by *Performer* magazine. Artists demanded payment for matinées and for playing twice nightly, and the big circuits responded by digging in their heels. Theatres were picketed and audiences witnessed the unusual spectacle of favourite stars, such as Marie Lloyd giving impassioned speeches in the street.

streets from lorries, cabs, and even from the kerb.

'At those places which were kept open, strange little programmes were provided, made up of all sorts and conditions of comparatively minor turns, aided and abetted by sundry concert artistes, and even by many a raw beginner.'

Even without the additional problems of menageries in the dressing room corridors, the atmosphere backstage was always hectic. Acts playing two and three halls a night arrived with only minutes to spare before going on, but the great treadmill of entertainment seldom faltered. *The Golden Penny*, a popular magazine of the day, gave a rare glimpse of pre-war Variety behind the scenes: 'Standing and watching the arrival of each artist, one sees what a serious business the entertaining of the public has become. Here is a man of short stature and

**Above and below** The Fredericks Troupe.

Ava, Zebra and Vora.

ordinary appearance; he is followed by a dresser and the stage hands, who lumber through the narrow passage with an enormous box. This is opened and all manner of wearing apparel turned out – wigs, coloured coats, armour and many other things. The man hurriedly disrobes before a small piece of mirror, while the dresser stands by with wig, coat, pants and paint. The music plays while the vermilion is being rubbed on the nose in handfuls, as if all modern humour culminated in that point. Then comes a jump in the air, and the funny man is ready for his patrons.

'The chatter behind ceases, or rather is drowned by the roar of welcome. He must be funny now, and on his hurried and perspiring return it is easy to see how far he has succeeded. A rush to the mirror to snatch off his present costume, only to substitute something much more extravagant, and he has gone again. At the end of the refrain he is heard literally throwing himself about the stage. This time the popular verdict is unmistakeable, and after exchanging a few commonplaces with those around him, he leaves to complete his rounds, and another performer takes his place.

'A celebrated "serio-comic" now arrives in all her make-up from her last turn; then comes a well-known comedian in burnt cork, and with a strong American accent. And so they continue until midnight. The rush and bustle, the desperate earnestness of it all never abates. . .'

It was not uncommon to have up to two dozen acts on a bill – sheer volume was one way of pulling the customers in. The dresser's timing had to be almost as good as the performer's and, when something went wrong, he was expected to improvise. Jimmy Murphy, a variety dresser on the Northern circuits before leaving for America to work as Stan Laurel's valet, frequently had his resources stretched to the limit.

He worked for Peg Leg Bates, a black American hoofer who could tap dance and somersault with great agility, despite having had his right leg amputated. Bates toured with a leather case of neatly packed spare wooden legs, each painted in a different colour. When the force of his dancing plunged one of them straight through a rotten stage floor in the West Country, he managed to extricate himself and continue his buck and wing with barely a flicker. But when the whole case went missing while changing trains for London, Jimmy had to find a solution. He caught the first train back to Lancashire and asked his old neighbour, Mr Walton the undertaker, to fashion a spare set. The coffin-maker worked all night on his lathe beneath his sign ('You may roam the whole world over – but I'll nail you in the end') and completed the task by daybreak. Jimmy breathlessly caught the next train back just in time for the show.

A DRESSER's job could be demanding, even exhausting work for speciality acts. Henry Lee, an American quick-change artist who delighted Edwardian audiences with costume impersonations of twenty characters in less than thirty minutes, went into strict training for his performances, and expected his dressers to do the same. He gave up smoking, exercised daily and ate nothing from midday until after his evening performance. His wardrobe, in pre-World War I days, cost more than £5,000, and he spent two and a half hours in the dressing room, marshalling his crew and preparing for his act.

A profile of 'the architect of men' in *Pearson's Magazine* gave a taste of the well-oiled, backstage pandemonium during his act. It was a classic piece of florid on-the-spot journalism that readers loved: 'In the dressing room three men and a girl flit silently hither and thither, like enormous butterflies hovering over flowers of various costumes. There is a rip here, and a tear there, a snip snip somewhere else as the nimble fingers mend the damage that is done from time to time. On a long counter there is a procession of wigs and properties, a vanguard of paints and powders, a squad of puffs and rabbits' feet, a regiment of towels and dusters – all in orderly array. What do you want? A No.4 greasepaint? There it is, third on the right. A Bismarck moustache? Top right hand corner – Mr Lee is a martinet.

'Myriads of chairs, upon each one a complete suit or uniform, line the walls; upon the floor, a battalion of boots and shoes. The outer crusts of Dickens, Salisbury, Gladstone and many others, limp and nerveless, waiting for the master-mind to create and resurrect them. Soon he comes and, whether clad or stripped, stands brawny and muscular as any athlete.

'And no athlete does more work than Mr Lee. There is no rest between turns for him, no time to regain his wasted breath – his assistants do not fan or sponge him, but instead fall simultaneously upon him, four to one, and twist and maul him within an inch of this life. Those three able-bodied men spring to the attack, rip off his Papal vestments and seemingly endeavour to flay the poor old man alive. You should see a pair of trousers flicker past you in the light, spring madly at his feet and, with a wild leap upward, clothe his legs. You should see the swish of the towel as it blots out Pope Leo, the sweeping gestures that paint in the next character in the series. You should see it all, I say, as with a frenzied pull the tunic enveloped him, the wig goes on with a slap, the beard is set, the face assumes a different expression, the door opens for him, the orchestra strikes up the Russian national anthem, and the Tsar of all the Russias commences his clever speech. The whole place is a whirl from beginning to end.

'The quick-change artist's life is not a happy one – you spend vitality and nerve tissue by the treble handfuls – your heart leaps to 104; and snatching men from beneath a falling chimney-stack is a leisurely occupation when compared with the work crammed into the space of twenty minutes.'

It was, as they say, a funny way to be a hero. While Robert Lee panted and perspired through his costume changes, a slim dark-haired lady called Vonetta had perfected a much faster act apparently single-handed. To make it more intriguing she changed on stage – behind a modesty screen, naturally. Audiences between 1906 and 1914 were completely baffled by 'The Only Lady Illusionist, Protean and Quick-Change Artiste.' Vonetta made her entrance in a gentleman's evening suit and slipped behind the screen to reappear seconds later dressed as a flamenco dancer. In the course of no more than a few minutes she made twenty-four completely different costume changes, offering £500 to anyone who could prove that she used a double. No one took up the challenge, but it is unlikely that her changes could have been made without the help of a highly-skilled dresser behind the screen.

If Variety was the spice of life, there has never since been quite such a proving ground for the apprentice performer. Backstage conditions in Edwardian days were spartan, despite the number of comparatively new theatres. Dressing rooms were gloomy, lit often only by a single gas mantle – or, in the better theatres, electric light – and with few facilities. The young performers who joined the exodus to America and moved into films found themselves working in luxury, but Variety became poorer without their energy and talent. Those who scorned the cinema and stayed on the circuits became a handful of familiar faces topping the bills around the country and, despite their popularity, more and more people were won over by the novelty and ever-changing action of the screen.

CHARLIE CHAPLIN assembled his tramp character from many experiences round the halls. His comedy timing owes a lot to Fred Karno, and other aspects were acquired on the road. According to Ethel Turner-Dauncey, his old school teacher from London, Chaplin 'copied his famous walk from an old man who gave oatmeal and water to horses in cabs and carts outside the Elephant and Castle.' The baggy trousers almost certainly came from a sketch he played as a teenager – Sam Cohen the Jewish Comedian. But the tramp walk, with its shrug, shuffle and skipping step were more than likely picked up from factory hand John Willie Jackson, of Golborne, near Warrington. He offered Charlie a job with his Eight Lancashire Lads, who specialized in comedy clog-dancing, and taught him the characteristic Lancashire steps.

By 1906, Chaplin was appearing in Casey's Court, a show based on the antics of a gang of cheeky Cockney kids who lived down an East End alley. One of his solo spots was a merciless send-up of stage healer Dr Walford Bodie, of whom more shortly. Stan Laurel was also among the cast of thirty youngsters run by Will Murray, and it was at a performance of

Charlie Chaplin in *City Lights*.

Casey's Court that the pair were spotted by Fred Karno, who was always on the lookout for rising talent.

Time has reduced the audiences, who saw the early British stars of Hollywood when they were music hall unknowns, to a dwindling handful. Those with fresher memories, in the peace following World War I, looked back on the glittering heyday of Variety with affection. Shaw Desmond recalled seeing the young Charlie Chaplin as a working turn in Fred Karno's Mumming Birds, before the company sailed for America. Karno took the show to New York for an eight week season and it ran, on and off, for nine years.

'Mumming Birds was a representation of the interior of a music hall,' Desmond said, 'and the little man in question used to enact the part of an inebriated swell with a violently encarmined nose, seated in a stage box. The way this drunken one would fall head foremost out of his box and hang there like a hairpin without smashing his features or crashing to the floor was to all of us consternation. The way in which he could be gloriously, riotously drunk in such a manner as no mortal ever was, without giving offence, was flusterbation. And the way in which he fell out of his box and removed his dress coat to display a flannel shirt and a dickey which, with false cuffs, was the everyday standby of the period, was a revelation.

'Then presently there strides on the stage a burlesque wrestler "The Terrible Turkey", all bulging muscles, hair a-bristle. There he stands, to challenge the world. The swell falls out of his box, this time successfully, and approaches. They grapple and fall. The swell, by a lurch and a hiccup, gets on top. The Turkey remains immovable whilst the swell ponders deeply the problem of the recumbent Ottoman. Bright idea! He bends down and tickles the Turk in the small ribs. "The Turkey" lets out a convulsive giggle and turns over to fall with his shoulder blades on the mat,

whilst the swell lurches triumphantly back to his box.

'He is unique. His star will set someday, and others will rise. But there will never be another Charlie, any more than there will be another Dan Leno or another Marie Lloyd.'

Chaplin was playing the same part in America in 1910 when Mack Sennett spotted him and later telegraphed a £25-a-week offer to join his Keystone Film Company. The little man accepted the job, even though the cable was addressed to Charles Chapman Esq. Sennett may not have had a memory for names, but his eye for talent was unerring.

Chaplin's understudy in the drunk sketch was a pale, wide-eyed youth called Stan Laurel, who had sailed with the Karno company aboard the *S.S. Cairnrona* in 1910. Mumming Birds – intended as a send-up of the old London Alhambra – was originally called Twice Nightly. Then, to cash in on the success of Karno's other shows, Jail Birds and Early Birds, its name was changed. He bought the script for £5, added his own touches, and installed comedian Fred Kitchen as lead in most of the sketches.

Many comics, including Max Miller, Flanagan and Allan, Billy Bennett and Sandy ('Can you hear me, mother?') Powell served their time as underpaid unknowns in Karno's travelling sweatshop. The maestro was a tough, curly-haired former West Country plumber whose real name was Fred Westcott. All his early productions were mostly mime, billed as Fred Karno's Speechless Comedians. The strict timing and precise visual comedy he insisted upon turned out to be the ideal training ground for silent films. Chaplin and Laurel, under his tuition, became popular slapstick comedians in early Variety, though their individual names were probably mostly unknown.

'I do not claim to have made Chaplin in any sense,' Karno said in later years. 'What

I do claim is that I put the lad on the right road and fanned the glow of his genius until it flamed.'

Karno, at one time, had fourteen shows on the road and made an enormous amount of money, which he poured into a folly in the middle of the Thames. The 'Karsino' – a weekend holiday resort with tennis courts, a golf course and restaurant – cost £70,000 to build on Taggs Island near Hampton Court. The official opening, on a windy May Sunday in 1913, sparkled with all the razmatazz of publicity that he loved. Jack Hylton's band played the latest dance tunes and the stars turned up in their hundreds. It was the biggest gathering of Variety and theatrical clans since the Royal Command Performance the year before. Food was plentiful, the drinks were endless and every newspaper in Britain found room to carry the story. But the Karsino was doomed. Fred had staged everything except the weather; Taggs Island struggled to tread water during the austere years of war, and when peace finally came the rain fell on every holiday season until he was declared bankrupt. He retired quietly to the Dorset seaside village of Parkstone, where he ran a wine and spirit shop until his death in 1947. The man who had banked £600 a week in the great days of Variety left £42.

Karno's flair for publicity was never equalled. To promote Jail Birds in 1901 he bought a black maria from Wandsworth Prison for £10 and drove it through London: 'A comic who played a policeman was the coachman; two others dressed as warders hung behind. Of the cast of twenty or more, those who could not get into the black maria followed in a wagonette wearing broad-arrow costumes,' *The Humorist* reported. 'It became a feature of London street life, but the lot of the bobby on the box was not a happy one, for in the rougher districts the people would lie in wait and wipe off old scores against the Force by pelting him and the warders with refuse.'

Karno's stunts were conceived with the simplicity and genius that sparked the best visual comedy of the period. As a touring impresario taking his working turns around the halls, his creative talent became totally immersed in the theatre; but by coincidence it was also finely tuned to the comedy reels being produced by Hollywood directors. A favourite publicity drive in the provinces, for instance, was to send four comedians – two dressed as convicts handcuffed to two dressed as prison warders – to a town a few miles away. There, they would board a return train – always at lunchtime when the streets were crowded – and stage a violent struggle outside the station.

The prisoners would make a break for freedom through the town centre pursued by the guards and, invariably, a crowd of several hundred onlookers. Predictably, the chase always ended at the doors of the theatre where tickets for the show just happened to be available. Karno, standing to one side, viewed the action as critically as if it were a stage production. 'Sweet are the uses of advertisement,' he was fond of murmuring when everything went according to plan.

His diversions livened the drab streets of Northern towns, and were such a clever soufflé of fear, excitement and amusement that few realized they were stage-managed and re-run regularly throughout the tour. In Wigan, local newspapers were full of a 'disaster' caused by a captive balloon which became ensnared in the tram wires (during the rush hour, naturally). The huge balloon, purchased cheaply somewhere on his travels, bore the slogan Fred Karno's Speechless Comedians. The crew tinkered feverishly beneath the basket with spanners, only to watch in horror as it rose into the overhead tram wires. Traffic was forced to a standstill and 5,000 workers, emptying local mills and factories for the lunchbreak, blocked the town centre watching the fun.

When the Duke of Cambridge died, Karno could not resist making an offer for his two gilded state coaches, complete with decorated harnesses and trappings. He bought them for £50 each, hired eight grey horses and costumes for six footmen and coachmen. Karno, dressed immaculately, set off in the first coach for a tour of West End watering holes – Claridge's, the Carlton, the Ritz – followed by two broken-down swells in the second coach, complete with bent top hats, torn opera cloaks and fingers poking through their gloves. At each halt the management rolled the red carpet across the pavement. Fred led the way, bowing graciously as the ingratiating smiles froze at the sight of his threadbare companions.

The essence of Mumming Birds, indeed all his shows, was an element of impending disaster. Audiences expected everything to go wrong at any minute, and of course it did, with well-planned precision. 'It is based on an idea as old as the hills,' Karno said, 'the essential cruelty of audiences, right from the days when the patrons in the Coliseum at Rome turned down their thumbs if the entertainment did not please them. Dud performers deserve the bird, and where I gambled on a certainty was in engaging accomplished professional artists to portray the supposedly incapable entertainers.

'Of course, when once the sketch took the public fancy the artists grasped the idea thoroughly and were enthusiastic. Not all audiences, though, understood that this was supposed to represent a diabolical programme of complete duffers. At Lincoln I remember they sat in solid and stolid silence, and another sketch actually had to be substituted after the Monday night.

'In Wakefield one sharp critic said: "Eh, ah never saw such a lot o' duds. Why, there were a feller there as was supposed to be balancing a ladder on his nose, an' you can believe me, I could see t'wire as was holdin' it up. Ay, an' a bit of a lass came out to sing – I neer heered anything like it. Our Maggie could ha' beaten 'em holler. An' as for t'conjuror chap – why t' bloomin' rabbits and pigeons an' things fair fell out of his pockets. . . They must think we're all daft i' Wakefield."

'On this burlesque stage, one character, the manager, was supposed to introduce each act as it appeared. He wore the accepted garb of the old-time music hall chairman; that is to say a very ill-fitting evening dress suit with a crimson silk handkerchief coyly tucked into the shirt-front. A lady in Huddersfield said: "It's a shame the way them artists are underpaid. Look at yon poor chap – you can see his shirt between his waistcoat and his trousers, an' he wears hob-nailed boots!"'

Billy Bennett, one of the Karno boys who graduated to become one of Variety's funniest comedians, retained the uniform and turned it into a trademark which lasted for the whole of his career and contributed to his fame. Stan Laurel looked back on his Karno days from the heights of Hollywood with fond memories: 'There was no-one like him,' he said. 'He had no equal. His name was box office. He was a great boss, kindly and considerate – and I hate to remember how he turned out eventually . . . it was a real tragedy.'

STAN LAUREL never lost his passion for the simple, visual fun of his Karno touring days. His California home, Fort Laurel, had windows fitted by studio special-effects men so that the weather could alternate from rain to blizzards at the touch of a button, to the consternation of guests. The unwary were also startled by the Laurel patent lavatory, which had an unnerving habit of sinking to the floor whenever anyone sat upon it. Visitors who emerged ruffled, but tight-lipped could expect more surprises in the course of the evening. Above the bar there was a life-size portrait of the great man

Stan Laurel and Oliver Hardy.

himself, with eyes which could be discreetly removed from a secret room behind it. Stan dispensed drinks generously and, as soon as a guest showed signs of having one too many, he would make an excuse and slip away to stand behind the painting. Alone at the bar, they would have the unsettling experience of watching the eyes in the portrait roll around and wink at them.

Stan originated from a terraced street in working class Ulverston, where industrial Lancashire climbs towards the pure air of Lakeland mountains. It somehow imbued him with a heady, rebellious streak which he could not resist exercising, even among the shockable wealthy of Beverly Hills. At more than one dinner party he concealed a small rubber hot water bottle, filled with vegetable soup, inside the armpit of his jacket. Half way through the meal he would finger his collar and, on the point of apparent collapse, mumble weakly that something was wrong with the food. Then he would suddenly jack-knife double and 'vomit' on to his plate, squeezing out the

soup with alarming force. In the stunned silence which inevitably followed Stan would recover a little and continue his meal, absent-mindedly picking up a soup spoon and politely sipping the appalling mess on his plate. Revolting in the extreme but, in many ways, pure Fred Karno.

While Oliver Hardy spent most of his off-screen hours playing golf, Stan took a delight in elaborate practical jokes, with Jimmy Murphy as his stooge. Chaplin enjoyed moving in sophisticated circles and dining in stylish Hollywood restaurants, where he loved to make a performance of preparing and tossing his own salads at the table.

'Stan was always irritated by pretentiousness,' Murphy says. 'At the time, he was not on speaking terms with his old pal, and decided to take him down a peg or two. He waited until he knew Chaplin was dining at a particular restaurant and drove me there with a car full of props. Stan walked in grandly, sat at a table in the centre of the room and called "Waiter!" I walked in on cue to take his order, and returned dragging a large tin bath-tub full of cabbages, potatoes, beetroot and other vegetables. Stan then proceeded to chop them up on the table with a cleaver. Then he ordered me to put them in the bath, pour a gallon of vinegar over them and trample them in my bare feet. Chaplin, surrounded by his friends at another table, was fuming. Stan ate some of his special salad to applause from the customers and the annoyance of the restaurant owners.'

Murphy's madcap valet career, incidentally, almost came to an end when he was dining out with his drinking buddy, Sabu the Elephant Boy, in the Clover Club, which was owned by Bugsy Siegel, a mobster with a murderous temper. Siegel, a member of the Jewish-Italian organized crime operation known as the Syndicate, and a member of Murder Incorporated, imposed his psychotic personality on the club. When an actor crawled under Siegel's table to give him a 'hotfoot' – holding a lighted match under his shoe – Jimmy laughed too loud and too soon.

Siegel ploughed a path to his table and promptly knocked out Murphy's front teeth with a pistol butt. Jimmy, a small roly-poly character, straight from the pages of Damon Runyon, retaliated instinctively with a 'Lancashire shuffle', which approximately involves a firm grip on the antagonist's testicles, followed by a butt on the nose.

'He was pretty mad and bit half my ear off,' Jimmy, now seventy-seven, recalls. 'Sabu and I took off through the kitchens. Siegel loosed a couple of bullets after us – I heard them ricochet – but we were too fast for him. At the back of the place we hid behind some garbage cans while they searched around for us. Victor Mature, who was helping them, spotted us and called out to Bugsy. We fell into Sabu's little M.G. Tourer and got the hell out.'

The sequel to this engaging tale, which unfortunately takes us too far from Variety to explore further, was that Stan and Ollie took Jimmy to their own dentist and treated him to a set of false teeth. They had the plate engraved 'Property of Laurel and Hardy Productions' and, with a classic Laurel touch, made Murphy sign a certificate stating that, if he ever left their employment, he would have to hand them back.

I N ADDITION to simple humour, Edwardians loved unusual working turns and greeted any form of novelty or originality with enthusiastic applause. Topical songs always had a good reception and, capitalizing on this, a new breed of quick-witted performers emerged – the *improvisatores*. They guaranteed to invent a rhyme based on any word the audience cared to call out and, like calypso

Jimmy Murphy.

singers, had to think on their feet. Half the fun was trying to catch them out and one trouper almost came to grief when a wag in the stalls shouted 'Mesopotamia!'

'At first the rhymer looked startled,' Chance Newton recalled. 'He was certainly a very illiterate, though smart fellow, and evidently that word was a bit beyond him. Soon, however, he pulled himself together and, stalking gravely towards the foot-lights, addressed the audience. "Ladies and gentlemen, a party in the stalls has given me the word Mesopotamia. But I beg to state —" and here he assumed a very reverential air — "that I never rhyme on Scriptual subjects!"'

Datas the Memory Man was another eccentric act who reinforced Fred Karno's belief that even the nicest audience has a vicious streak. There were countless attempts to catch him out, but no record of any succeeding. Datas, who rejoiced in the real name of Harry Bottles, was a gas works employee who had made the most of a long illness by memorizing historical dates from an old encyclopedia. He soon found that he could recite all the past Derby winners in reverse order, the reigns of British monarchs and details of every ship that had sunk in English waters. An agent who overheard him answering questions at the bar of a London pub, booked him into a Pimlico theatre for a week. Eighteen months later he was still there. Datas wore a flat cap and choker and puffed on a cigarette while reeling off dates of major earthquakes and F.A. Cup winners. He dealt only in dates, but apparently had a capacity to absorb all kinds of statistical information.

When an army officer in the audience asked out of the blue if there were more acres of land in Yorkshire than letters in the Bible, Datas faltered and insisted that he only knew dates. When the man pushed his point, Datas broke his rule and told him: 'There are 3,800,000 acres in Yorkshire and 3,500,000 letters in the Bible. And if you don't believe me sir, you go away and count them!'

Pre-war variety audiences had inherited a Victorian fascination with the macabre, a point not overlooked by theatre managers who would stage anything to draw crowds. In Hull they queued to see every-day items belonging to Dr Crippen's wife Belle in 1911, just as their grandparents had watched 152 kg (24 st) Arthur Orten, the fraudulent claimant to the Titchbourne fortune, exhibit himself round the halls on his release from a ten-year prison sentence. Variety became a showcase for a madcap range of attractions; anything which might remotely intrigue or tittilate found its place. Geoff Mellor, an expert on Northern music hall, tells of Sacco the Fasting Man, a Kafkaesque character whose dubious bills claimed that he had fasted for fifty days. Audiences paid an extra tuppence on top of their admission fee to see him at Hull. Excessive movement was not Sacco's speciality, and he appears to have done little apart from waste away in a loin cloth, but business at the Hippodrome was so unexpectedly brisk that the management quickly raised the price to sixpence on the pretext that he was 'sinking fast'. Sacco, however, seems to have possessed remarkable reserves, as he lived to publicly fade again at a hall on the other side of town a week later.

The flamboyant Dr Walford Bodie sur-passed every theatre manager's expecta-tions by performing miracles of healing on stage, twice nightly. He wore an immacu-late top hat and, twirling his waxed mous-tache, wired sick volunteers to primitive electrical apparatus (at fourteen he was an apprentice electrician with the National Telephone Company) to demonstrate theatrical 'cures'. His career as a working turn was understandably short-lived — Bodie miracles were so sensational that he soon played to capacity audiences wherever he went. 'The Most Remarkable Man On Earth, The Great Healer, The

Modern Miracle Worker, Demonstrating Nightly Hypnotism, Bodie Force and the Wonders of Bloodless Surgery,' was among the more modest of his advertisements. He lived up to his claims, assisted by his wife 'Princess Rubie', 'Mystic Marie' (his sister) and 'La Belle Electra' – and no one quite discovered how. He began his stage career as a ventriloquist operating ten identically-dressed dummies, but the day he obtained a dubious American university degree, probably purchased, he was on the threshold of a forty-year career in 'Electric Wizardry'. By 1906 he was supplementing his £400 a week income by marketing jars of 'Bodie's Electric Liniment' in the foyer. He claimed to have cured 900 cases of paralysis diagnosed untreatable by London hospitals, but not all who paid to see him watched in admiration. In 1912 a party of irate medical students invaded Glasgow Coliseum and smashed his equipment on stage.

The audience, of course, loved it, and managements even more so. 'His cures of paralysis by means of massage, electricity and hypnotic suggestions have been the wonder of the world, and have been patronized by clergy, medical men and the élite of society in every part of the Kingdom,' the *Variety Theatre Annual* for 1906 recorded. 'Moreover, he has been the means of drawing to our music halls a class of people who have never before entered their portals, and who, in all probability, would never have done so had it not been for the fame of his miracles – beg pardon – the "doctor" emphatically rejects the idea of anything miraculous. Everything he does, he claims, can be explained by natural scientific means.' Away from the rough and tumble of the stage the 'doctor' threw noisy parties on his floodlit Thames houseboat, *La Belle Electra*. At the age of sixty, after the death of his wife, he married Florrie, an attractive twenty-two year old chorus girl.

Bodie represented the handful of bizarre turns who reached the top of the bill, but there were many others who earned a lucrative living touring variety theatres with speciality acts. *Lost Empires* producer June Howson had a distant uncle, Brinn, whose strong-man act was a great draw at the turn of the century. Brinn's performance always had a strong patriotic theme, which boosted his popularity as war approached. He juggled with heavy artillery shells, balancing them end to end on the tip of an iron rod, and catching them one by one on the nape of his neck. His assistants, dressed as soldiers and sailors, marched around handing him props against the painted backdrop of a battleship. His *tour de force* was balancing on the tip of his chin a platform which supported a naval rating firing a deck gun, accompanied by much Union Jack waving.

For sheer showmanship he was eclipsed only by Eugene Sandow, a good-looking German gymnast who billed himself as The Strongest Man In The World. At the Royal, in Holborn, he astounded audiences by lifting a 142 kg (312 lb) iron weight with one hand – the most anyone had previously attempted was a 113 kg (250 lb) dumb-bell. Sandow enhanced his reputation further by the almost unbelievable feat of lifting a 267 kg (42 st) dray horse with one hand on the stage of the Tivoli. The undoubted king of the strongmen had a 127 cm (50 in) chest and was regarded by awed Edwardians as 'the Modern Hercules and the Perfect Man' . . . even if he wasn't British. He performed in bronze body make-up, wearing tights and a strategically-placed fig leaf; he built up a profitable side-line advertising cocoa.

None of his audiences knew what to expect next when he strode on stage to warm up with muscle-flexing poses – he fought a lion which had eaten its keeper only a few days earlier, and lifted both a concert pianist and his grand piano with one hand. The musician continued to play stirring selections from famous pieces throughout his ordeal. By 1914, Sandow had made enough to open his own gym and sell body-building courses. Despite his fitness, years of lifting progressively heavy weights took their toll. He suffered a heart attack in middle age while trying to lift his car from a country ditch.

Those without Sandow's strength and dedication to physical culture relied on dexterity to earn a living. Take, for example, acts like the Elliots, who managed to astutely combine stage bicycles with the wonders of electricity. Their set, which caused enormous transport problems, was wired with 1000 bulbs, an attraction itself before World War I, and was littered with fifty musical instruments, including three fairground organs, which they also played between pedalling round the stage. It was perhaps a sign of the times that acts could build to such eccentric proportions as audiences hungered for fresh amusement until, by the outbreak of war, some had evolved into a patchwork of surreal juxtapositions. The El Granadas, a rope-spinning, whip-cracking act, had also been part of a team of sixteen acrobats, all dressed as Royal Scots Guards who pedalled furiously on trick cycles in military formation. Bicycles and electricity were, of course, a great novelty, almost as popular on stage as in the streets – Auntie (the comedian P. L. Clark) for instance, worked steadily from 1911 right through the war years dressed as a cycling panto dame. However, when they became commonplace many speciality performers were forced to change with the times and search for more unusual material.

Among those who opted to stick with a safe formula for years, milking it with a gusto possible only in the years before television demanded a constant source of fresh material, were Wilson, Kepple and Betty. Their sand dance, still fondly remembered, ran for decades until the decorative Betty left to devote her talents to journalism.

THE HIGH POINT of Music Hall and emerging Variety was the Royal Command Performance of 1912, the first for a variety show, and graced by a jewelled assembly of long-forgotten European Royalty. The Palace Theatre was garlanded for the occasion like an English flower garden, with the Royal box, for the King and Queen, decorated in the shape of a rose bower. There was a Russian grand duchess, three princesses of Schleswig-Holstein (though what they made of it, no one could guess) the Duke, Duchess and Prince of Teek, a Battenberg princess and Prince Arthur of Connaught. It was Music Hall's magnificent and elaborate farewell. Ahead lay the Great War and less intimate forms of entertainment. The best artists gathered for what would be the end of an era, including juggler Cinquevalli, Harry Tate, Harry Lauder, G. H. Chirgwin, George Robey, Little Tich and Vesta Tilley. By the end of a show which lasted several hours, not without incident, they had raised £2,738 for music hall charities.

The vast line-up of stars were outnumbered by those who were disappointed at not having been chosen, posing a difficult problem for the organizers. A compromise was reached by ending the show with a mass finale of more than 150 artists singing *God Save The King*, led by baritone Harry Claff dressed in a white suit of armour. For months afterwards, Harry and others who appeared in the show, brashly cashed in on the honour across their billboards. Music hall performers are affectionately remembered as having hearts of gold, but when it came to business many of the big names had minds of steel and hearts like cash registers.

There was one omission from the programme, so obvious that no one even dared mention the name. Marie Lloyd, synonymous with the people's entertainment, and undoubtedly the most famous lady of her day, was pointedly not invited,

*Charivari* song-sheet.

even to the finale which was supposed to represent the best of Music Hall. The reason, which everyone knew, was that Marie's performance was considered a little near the knuckle for polite society, and highly unsuitable for Royal company. Marie felt affronted by the over-protective attitude of the powerful theatre owners who made up the Command Performance selection committee, and admitted privately that she was hurt by it. But, in the best tradition of showmanship, she bounced back by insisting that, henceforth, all her bills bore the strap-line 'The Queen of Comediennes'.

The Royal Command Performance itself proved that snubbing Marie was perhaps not as foolish as it seemed. In an age of propriety it was surprising, particularly by our standards, how the most innocent incidents could give public offence. Before the first half had drawn to a close, consternation rippled through the Royal box when Queen Mary was heard to order that 'the gaze of the ladies be not directed at the stage.' Fans fluttered and a whisper ran through the stalls like a wall of cards. The cause of the commotion was Vesta Tilley, strutting on stage dressed as a man. Palpitations lasted throughout her performance of *Algy, The Piccadilly Johnny* and, though the show ended without further controversy, the scene remained a talking point for weeks.

Music Hall – risqué though it was, unashamedly sentimental at times, and fond of poking a roisterous finger at the class divide – celebrated a uniquely British brand of humour. Its targets were toffs and swells, innocent provincials wondering at the sights of London, nagging wives and drunken husbands – caricatures in which audiences recognized something of themselves. Ragtime, and other American fashions, created a shift in humour. It became broader, slicker, and in doing so lost some of its Englishness – the blank look, the knowing wink, the arrogant strut, the stance which summoned a dozen familiar images.

The great move to revue, which wooed a few of the well-known music hall stars, featured sparkling casts of singing, dancing bright young things, in a format which became a template for modern entertainment. Salty humour was edged out by wit and satire: clever stuff for cosmopolitan audiences who preferred to laugh at others, rather than the wry look at themselves which was the stuff of Music Hall. The coster and the Lancashire lad, the Cockney sparrow and Fred Karno slapstick appeared coarse against the waspish elegance of Noel Coward and the sophisticated melodies of George Gershwin. In the carefree years of revue which followed 1918, the drawing room took over from the street corner as the milieu of fashionable entertainment.

One of Music Hall's great traditions was that star names and working turns alike invariably came on with a song. Today it has become little more than a useful device to guillotine the gags, change the mood and exit safely. However, the importance of songs in everyday life has not diminished, as the millions of hours radio stations devote to them indicates. Variety comedians were known for their catch-phrases, but their essential trademark song helped even more to convey their powerful stage personalities. Rather like children who can beg for the same bedtime story again and again without tiring of it, audiences could not let their favourite star go until they had heard his song. They sang the choruses along with him, swaying in their seats, as though each familiar rendering added to its magic.

The great watershed of World War I brought a boredom threshold which dropped with successive generations. Cinema, and ultimately television, sharpened a public need for constant change. Home and work alike became filled with disposables, and along with these fundamental changes, the life of the popular song became progressively shorter. Audiences, of course, still expect performers to sing their favourite numbers, but there has been a subtle change of attitude. Today we expect to be entertained – the crowds who clamoured for *My Old Dutch*, or *My Fiddle Is My Sweetheart*, felt reassured that their heroes still represented them and, like a spell repeated, life would somehow be better for each singing of the chorus.

Thomas Burke noticed this shift emphasis in *London In My Time* in 1934: 'If you are old enough to remember the London and suburban music halls you will be able to recall the spectacle of the crowd when it came out. It came out, or poured out, bubbling. It came out humming choruses. It came out with bright eyes. Watch the people coming from a movie palace. They come out frowning. They come out without speaking. They come out as though there were nothing in life worth living for. . .'

One of the side effects of television's immense contribution to the way we live has been to encourage a healthy cynicism about entertainment. It is hard to believe, eighty years on, that Edwardian audiences could pull out their handkerchiefs and openly sob at the lyrics of sentimental narrative songs. Street hawkers did a roaring trade in sheet music, and business was even brisker for cheap, pirated copies. Reading the lyrics today, for we no longer have an accurate idea of how they were performed, they appear sentimental, naïve and, above all, wholly predictable. But perhaps such cynicism says more about ourselves than the huge cross-section of society who enjoyed them in an age of innocence

*Keep Smiling* song-sheet.

which vanished abruptly with the war.

Some of the early music hall tear-jerkers were still being requested years later; temperance songs such as Elsa Lanchester's *Don't Go Out Tonight, Dear Father* was a classic of its kind about a father determined to have his pint with the boys, even though his wife is dying.

> Don't go out tonight, dear father;
> Think, oh, think how sad 'twill be
> When the angels come to take her,
> Papa won't be there to see.

The sentiment was suffocating, the lyrics banal, the story-line nauseatingly compulsive . . . but audiences adored them. Typical of the style was *A Stroke Of The Pen*, sung by Lottie Elliott and written just before the turn of the century, about a dad who had worked twenty-five years as a commissionaire in the County Bank.

> I shall never forget the story, how my dad
>   once saved a life.
> He was told to fetch a policeman, but he
>   brought a widowed wife.
> Quite a youth had sent a cheque up,
> Plainly forged another's name,
> And the cashier had detained him till his
>   widowed mother came.

> 'Madam, this youth, a few moments ago,
> Came and presented this cheque, you must
>   know.
> Is that *your* signature, please? Yes or no?'
> Then (every moment seemed ten),
> Then, with a burst of affection Divine,
> '*Yes*,' said the mother, '*that signature's mine!*'
> Saving her son from the stain of a crime,
> Risked by the stroke of a pen.

67

An honorable sentiment not without parallel today, the exception being that, once safely home, a modern mother would probably have half killed him.

Narrative songs of this calibre have a wincing quality, yet the tradition continues to surface from time to time in the form of truly awful records like Wink Martindale's *Deck Of Cards*, *Terry* by Twinkle and Jess Conrad's supremely dreadful *This Pullover* – curiously, all highly popular songs. By such standards we can hardly deride popular ballads enjoyed by Edwardians. Most of them rambled like an English country road, never seeming to get to the point, which was usually obvious from the first verse. Others had a lyrical abruptness bordering on shorthand, which still managed to convey the message. T. E. Dunville, who took his name from a whisky bottle, sang eccentrically succinct songs such as:

> Little boy
> Pair of skates
> Broken ice
> Heaven's gate.

Which prompted Max Beerbohm to ask in the *Saturday Review*, after seeing him in 1901, 'Who is this loathsome object?'

Variety raised the art of bathos to previously unknown heights. George Lashwood, 'The Beau Brummel Of The Halls', was something of a master of the descriptive song. His most famous was perhaps *After The Ball*, which was still being sung when he took his final bow in 1918. Audiences never seemed to tire of his patriotic ballads, such as *The Gallant Twenty-First* and *The Death And Glory Boys*, but his finest, or worst, achievement (depending on your point of view) was *The Cabman's Story* – the dramatic tale of a hansom cabbie picking his way through snow-bound London streets at midnight to collect a fare from an expensive hotel. As the stylish couple step into the cab. . .

> Jack looked upon the woman's face, then,
>   piercing like a knife,
> The awful truth came home to him – the
>   woman was his wife!

It is perhaps only fair to mention at this stage that the story gets progressively worse. . .

> He lifted the trap, and with blazing eyes
>   looked down on the pair inside,
> And he saw the face of his guilty wife,
>   pallid and terrified.
> 'As sure as God's in heaven, my girl, you
>   never shall fool me again.
> Say what prayers you may have to say; 'say
>   'em with all your might,
> For you and your cursed paramour are
>   riding to Hell tonight!'
>
> Little he cared for the pleading cry that rose
>   from the lips of his wife,
> Little he cared for the curses of the villain
>   who'd ruined her life.
> Faster and faster they raced along, waking
>   the echoes around.
> And the iron-shod hoofs of the galloping
>   horse lashed at the snow-white ground.

Eventually Lashwood would release the audience from its suspense with the last verse in which they all, cab and horse included, end up at the bottom of the icy Thames.

The least that can be said for these songs is that they are memorable. For the singers, however, this was never quite enough; they embellished their material with distinctive appearances – the swell, the rustic, the broken-down toff, or totally individual costumes and make-up.

GEORGE CHIRGWIN, The White-eyed Kaffir, was among the last of the burnt-cork minstrels who toured the halls. He had a remarkable falsetto voice, and sang with an emotional intensity which cast a silence over noisy audiences. The range of his

George Chirgwin.

voice was exceptional – many numbers were sung in an equally pure baritone. Chirgwin's costume, both comical and sinister, also set him apart from other performers. He wore black tights, which accentuated his thin legs, a black floor-length frockcoat swinging open like a ruffian's, and a two-foot high top hat reminiscent of a voodoo priest. His face was blacked-up, except for a large white diamond around his right eye. It was said that he stumbled on this dramatic patch when he accidentally wiped off his make-up before going on stage one evening. Occasionally, he would change to an all-white costume with a powdered white face and a black diamond around his eye. The effect was equally startling.

Chirgwin made his entrance slowly and deliberately, planting each black ballet shoe carefully in front of him. His towering topper covered the eye everyone waited to see, until he swung to face the audience full-on and threw back his head contemptuously to reveal the lurid diamond. At this moment the audience would erupt into thunderous applause, stamping feet, and a mass roar of 'Good old George!' He always carried a banjo, but occasionally played bagpipes or a one-stringed fiddle, from which he coaxed melancholy notes.

At the slightest hint that Chirgwin might sing *My Fiddle Is My Sweetheart*, a hush would fall over the audience. On a rare recording he made before retiring to buy a pub in Shepperton, his voice has an eerie quality, though the words are quite banal. As a performer, Chirgwin dominated his audience with his presence, breaking off between songs to stalk the stage answering their questions or commenting on the news.

> My fiddle is my sweetheart
> And I'm her only beau
> I take her by the waist like that
> Because I love her so. . .

Chirgwin was among the last of hundreds of burnt-cork minstrels who occupy a curious place in music hall history. The vogue for white entertainers singing songs of the American cotton fields in tortured accents reached its height in the mid nineteenth century. By Edwardian times their popularity had waned, but after the war there was a great revival of black music. 'There is hardly a tune of the moment without plantation origin,' *Sunday Times* columnist E. V. Lucas was to write in 1928. 'There are negro bands everywhere, while if you go to Drury Lane you will find the stage looking like a cotton field.'

The original black singer who spawned so many imitators is thought to have been Jim Crow, a Southern slave born in 1754, who ran away to New York and earned so much from his singing and agile dancing that he retired to his own farm in Virginia. A flood of 'Ethiopian entertainers' followed, eager for the freedom his flashing footsteps had won. They played banjo and bones, and wore frilled shirts, until a shrewd white man realized the possibilities of blacking his face and imitating them. Thomas Dartmouth Rice heard Jim Crow singing in the streets of Cincinnati in 1830 and, with the help of a borrowed porter's overalls, lifted the songs to use in his own act. Rice brought his enormously successful show to London's Surrey Theatre in 1836, when Thackeray was among the cheering audiences who called for more.

There were one or two comedians who parodied plantation songs in a derogatory fashion aimed at wringing a cheap laugh from the original singers; but most of the imitators were without racial malice and performed with great respect for their black predecessors. Burnt-cork artists such as Edwin P. Christy, who formed the popular Christy Minstrels, sang sentimental numbers like *Swanee River* and *My Old Kentucky Home* with warmth and seriousness. The ballads of Stephen Collins Foster, who wrote many highly successful minstrel songs, were a sentimental, sanitized version of plantation melodies, created for white audiences. In our times, when golliwogs and Enid Blyton books arouse passionate accusations of racism, it is difficult to imagine that the majority of blacked-up singers idolized the artists who inspired them. Young boys sat in their bedrooms practising the bones, and quickly learnt that burnt champagne corks yielded the best make-up.

'The present-day curtain rises on nothing that I can anticipate with a tenth of the joy that filled me when Christie was a name to make the heart beat faster,' E. V. Lucas recalled. By 1904, St James' Hall, 'London's Burnt-Cork Capital', had staged its last minstrel show. George Chirgwin, the White-eyed Kaffir, G. H. Elliot, the Chocolate-coloured Coon, and Eugene Stratton, the Dandy-coloured Coon, were among the last to sing and soft-shoe their gentle melodies until the style was rediscovered by another generation. The naïve enthusiasm of music hall audiences for such tasteless figures faded as people gained political awareness.

When immigration and international travel were in their infancy, the horizons of the average theatre-goer were rather more domestic than those of today, and political news at home became a favourite focus of variety songs. They found a popular platform in the end-of-pier pavilions and seaside concert huts, where holidaymakers, in a relaxed mood away from the cares of work, enjoyed a clever dig at the state of the nation. The Employer's Liability Act of 1906, for instance, produced the chorus:

> There's a sun still shining in the sky
> > (the sun is shining)
> Though to raise more money I must try
> > (a mortgage signing)
> As today a mouse made for the under
> housemaid
> And she fell downstairs and blacked her
> eye.
> > (she started pining)

> When my butler drank the cellar dry
> > (he's always wining)
> An annuity I had to buy,
> As he's left my service blind; now he's
> rich – but never mind. . .
> There's a sun still shining in the sky.

By 1914, the sound of carefree footsteps on shingle holiday beaches had been replaced by the tramp of marching feet. The great Edwardian concert party was over, and topical songs sought a new home in variety theatres, among people flocking to take a welcome break from the pressures of war or guarding home defences.

> I'm just an ordinary special constable.
> I pad the hoof from two am till six.
> My lonely beat is round about the water
> works,
> Just to see that no-one's up to any tricks. . .

For a short time the war threatened to decimate show business as the rush to enlist gained momentum. Famous names were caught in the confusion – George Edwardes, the imposing Irish 'guv'nor' of the Gaiety, was arrested and interned on holiday in Germany to be released, indignant but unbowed, months later. Stars such as Marie Lloyd and George Robey joined touring revues, of which there were almost a hundred on the road within the first six months of the war. Many understaffed theatres survived on this welcome new formula of only one star's wages to pay. Music Hall, with its full-blooded humour, had gone. Its replacement, Variety, was destined to be another passing show as Hollywood claimed the lion's share of audiences. Each new phase in the fickle history of entertainment reflected the spirit of the age which breathed life into it. As music hall historian W. Macqueen-Pope said: 'Every generation gets the theatre it wants. . . and deserves.'

# ALL DONE WITH MIRRORS

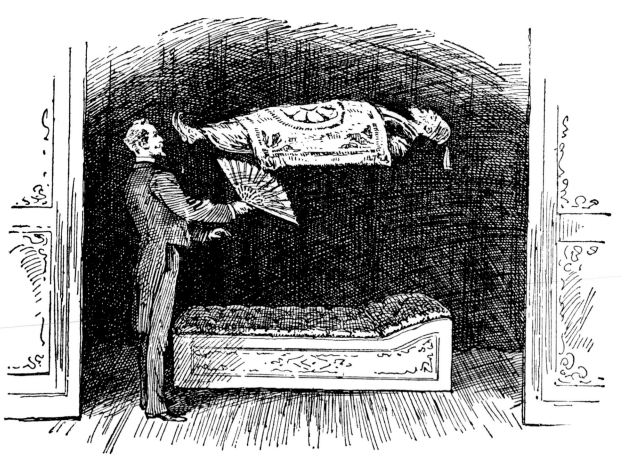

The celebrated 'levitation' mystery.

IT WAS REALLY not Mr Marsden's day. The leader of the orchestra at the Grand Theatre of Varieties, Stoke-on-Trent, limped back to his terraced house in Newcastle Lane at half past seven with his arm in a sling. The children were sent to bed while Mr Marsden explained his unexpected presence to his wife. The magician performing on stage, he told her somewhat painfully, had not required the orchestra for his final number, the Vanishing Lady. Only the drummer was called upon to supply the dramatic rolls and cymbal crescendos, so the wing-collared boys of the band trooped from the orchestra pit for a quiet smoke beneath the stage.

A few minutes later the red light flashed, signalling that the act was drawing to an end and they were required for the closing number. As they rose and dutifully ground their cigarette stubs into the floor, the trap-door high above them crashed open and the Vanishing Lady plunged on to Mr Marsden, completely flooring him. Three days later – there was no sick-pay in Variety – he was back at his music stand, playing the violin with great difficulty.

Mr Marsden died in 1910, but the story is still fondly remembered in his family. The magician's name has long been forgotten, but the incident was more than likely one of a catalogue of mishaps in his career. The theatre is one of those unfortunate places of work where the slightest mistake is magnified, exaggerated and, occasionally, remembered for generations. Magicians as a breed fear failure more than any other performer; fumbling fingers, a forgetful assistant or a stubborn trap-door bolt can mean the stigma of ridicule or, at worst, a lost booking.

Illusionists, by the demands of their profession, are an unhappy bunch. Their skills require hours of sombre dedication before a mirror, and a serious, often tetchy, approach to their work. They trust no one, preferring to examine and maintain their equipment personally; they cling to their secrets with a Scrooge-like tenacity. The team work of television has reduced the solitary nature of the craft, but it is unlikely that their outlook has changed. Priestley's Ganga Dun shared a conviction that magicians are superior to their audiences. They can deceive them with the speed of a flashing hand, distract them with the sight of a pretty girl and dazzle them with the aid of no more than a piece of elastic and a copious sleeve. And in many ways they were right; a good magician has the creativity of an engineer, the genius of a skilled mechanic and the dexterity of a surgeon. But, as they are all too keenly aware, the best trick, even in the most experienced hands, can go wrong.

Howard Thurston, a popular American illusionist who once sold meat tenderizers from a handcart in the street, stood by the magician's maxim: never admit a mistake. In one pre-World War I illusion, the Glass-lined Trunk, he guaranteed to produce a girl from an apparently empty box; but when the trunk was wheeled on stage and the sides opened to reveal the glass lining, it was far from empty. To Howard's horror, the girl was already reclining inside it.

In one of those moments prompted by inspiration and panic, he announced: "'One of the great signs of a magician is first to lead his audience to believe that they have discovered one of his secrets. This evening

I have taken the opportunity to try an experiment. Perhaps one half, or two-thirds, of you believe you have just seen the form of a young lady inside that trunk. The rest of you may not be certain what you saw. I'll prove to you that your eyes have deceived you ... the trunk is empty!"

'My assistants wheeled the trunk round,' Thurston recalled. 'Again it was opened, and seen to be empty. The audience gasped and, before the people had recovered from their astonishment, I had closed the trunk and had it wheeled around again. "Now," I resumed, "I will again prove that your eyes have deceived you. You're satisfied the trunk is empty ... Behold!" The trunk was swung open, and there lay the young lady.'

Thurston exited to great applause – and, presumably, a stiff brandy and a blazing row with his assistants. Harry Kellar, a brilliant illusionist who died from a 'flu attack in 1922, learned from experience never to depend on anyone, and insisted that each piece of his equipment was built twice as strongly as it needed to be.

Another Edwardian illusionist, Servais Le Roy, a Belgian who billed himself as The Devil In Evening Clothes, found himself facing the gravest nightmare dreaded by every magician – an acute shortage of rabbits. He was playing Milwaukee at the time and immediately hired a car to scour the surrounding countryside for a farm. After many hours Le Roy located a rundown homestead farmed by an old German *émigré*, and bought a large quantity of rabbits. He was so pleased with the purchase that he fished in his wallet for a free theatre pass for the old man and his wife, and presented it to them with his personal card. The farmer took one glance at the caricature of the devil in evening clothes engraved on it, snatched back the rabbits and slammed the door.

Few artists can go to work before an audience which is constantly on the look-

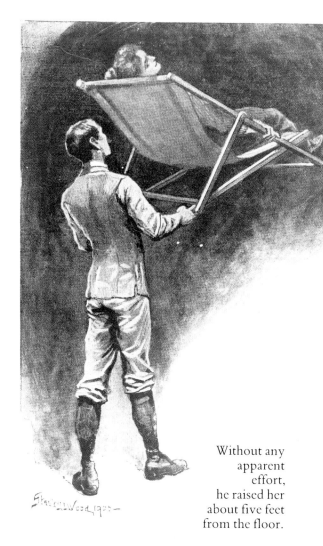

Without any apparent effort, he raised her about five feet from the floor.

out for the slightest slip and, with the mean streak inherent in human nature, half hoping that something will go wrong. Houdini, who began his career as an illusionist and became the world's greatest escapologist, was a brilliant amateur psychologist who traded on the frailties of his audience, manipulating their emotions to a point where tension crackled tangibly round the theatre. Some of his escapes were performed within seconds of being lowered into the box, and he would sit in the wings, or beneath the stage, sipping tea while anxiety stalked the auditorium.

Danger has always played an important role in successful illusions, but Edwardian stage magicians drew on a dimension which delved into deeper uncertainties. Spiritualism was a great topic of the day, viewed with a mixture of fear and suspicion, and many performers featured 'spirit cabinets', disembodied forms, levitation and other mumbo jumbo which gave the cult's simple followers a sinister reputation. Magic has essentially changed little since the fourteenth century; even with all the sophisticated production skills Paul Daniels can muster, its currency is still a sense of wonder and an element of risk.

CHUNG LING SOO combined the two in an act in which he swallowed burning rope and plunged his hands into boiling water to produce live hens. The main attraction, however, was his celebrated Catching The Bullet trick, which mystified Edwardians and ultimately led to his tragic death on stage at Wood Green Empire in 1918. To his audiences, Chung Ling Soo was the consummate Chinese magician in silk robes and pigtail, surrounded by props which exploded in clouds of smoke and popping firecrackers. Before each week's run he would stage a Press conference, speaking to reporters in Cantonese, which was translated by his assistant.

It was an elaborate façade which he managed to sustain throughout his career, and one which would have been impossible to maintain before later generations of hard-nosed newspapermen and television interviewers. Pre-war audiences happily swallowed Chung Ling Soo's exotic public image. Behind the brightly-coloured temple robes and oriental make-up he was, in fact, Bill Robinson, a miner's son from Blackburn who had developed a fascination for China and spent much of his time hanging around Nelson Street, Liverpool's Chinatown, observing manners and customs. That, at least, is one story. There is some confusion about his early life; other versions say he was born in New York, and he certainly lived in America for many years, where he acquired a distinctive drawl and a fondness for chewing gum.

The act on which Chung Ling Soo built his legendary reputation involved two marksmen aiming at his heart and firing marked rifle bullets, which he caught on a plate. The firearms, fitted with false barrels, were the key to the trick – old muzzle-loaders which required the powder and ball to be rammed down with a rod.

To his audiences, Chung Ling Soo was the consummate Chinese magician in silk robes and pigtail. . .

This action was vital to the illusion: the bullet dropped into a secret chamber in the ramrod holder, while the harmless powder and wadding went into the real barrel.

Chung Ling Soo was understandably wary of gunsmiths discovering his secret, and for many years insisted on servicing his own weapons. What he failed to realize was that an internal screw had corroded, allowing powder to trickle over a period, grain by grain, along the threads into the hidden chamber and lodge behind the musket ball. The gun, later examined for the East Middlesex coroner by Robert Churchill, a gunsmith from the Strand, was found to be at least twenty years old and the type traded by Persian gun-runners.

The trick had a doom-laden history well known to audiences. It was invented by Philip Astley, an English army officer, about 1780. When the secret leaked out and other magicians tried to duplicate it, the fatalities began. One of the earliest occurred on stage in Strasbourg, when an illusionist performed the trick in a William Tell tableau. The magician placed an apple on his son's head and fired a marked bullet into the core. That, at least, was the theory; but unfortunately the trick went wrong and the boy was killed. Then a conjuror named De Linsky attempted it at Arnstadt, Germany, in 1824 when a team of assistants, dressed as infantrymen, levelled their muskets at his wife. His secret was that, in biting the cartridges, the men were supposed to deftly remove the bullets with their teeth. One of them unfortunately neglected this vital point, and Madame De Linsky was shot dead before a horrified audience.

One of the most skilled of all stage magicians, Professor Anderson the Wizard of the North, whose career stretched thirty years from 1830, perfected the bullet-catching trick, which misfired on him on only one occasion. He always asked for a volunteer from the audience to fire the weapon at him. By a million to one chance the man he chose was acquainted with the trick, and refused to let Anderson touch the gun. He loaded it himself and coolly aimed at the centre of the Professor's chest, expecting him to call a halt to the performance. He underestimated Anderson's bravado. He had the showmanship of a real magician, and would not only never admit to a mistake, but realized that his reputation was at stake. The audience sensed that something unusual was taking place, but Anderson called the marksman's bluff and with granite flamboyance ordered him to open fire. The man hesitated, then laid down the gun and left the stage. Anderson appealed to his audience for a volunteer with more guts and, when someone else stepped forward, carried out the trick as it should have been performed.

Others, such as Robert-Houdin and Alexander Herrmann frequently presented the illusion without injury. Herrmann's staging was quite sensational. A squad of soliders, under the command of a sergeant, marched into the auditorium and lined up on a platform built in the middle of the theatre. Herrmann faced the firing squad from the stage, caught the marked bullets on a plate and immediately passed them round to be identified. Watching from the wings was his stage manager, a man called Bill Robinson who decided to launch his own act and use the illusion himself.

Years later, as Chung Ling Soo, he was building to the climax of his act before the second house on a Saturday night at Wood Green Empire. His wife Dot – otherwise Suee Seen – placed the bullets into a cup and took them into the audience to be marked. Powder had been hard to come by because of the war restrictions, but Robinson had had supplies sent to him by friends in the army. On stage, he paced dramatically up and down in his plumed warrior costume, while his assistants Dan Crowley and Jack Grossman displayed the guns. When the powder was rammed home, the house fell silent to a drum roll.

Chung Ling Soo, holding the plate in front of him, nodded the order to fire. But instead of the familiar clatter of balls rolling in the plate, he jerked backwards, managed to keep his feet for several paces, then fell to the floor. Crowley, who later told the coroner that he had felt the rifle kick unusually hard that night, was the first at his side. 'My God,' Robinson whispered, 'I've been shot – lower the curtain' – the last words he spoke in public. Twenty-four hours later he was dead from a gunshot wound in the right lung.

In the week which followed before the inquest, Dot weathered rumours that she had tried to murder him, or that Chung Ling Soo had staged a bizarre public suicide because he was in debt. The simple truth was that his obsession for secrecy had caused his equipment to deteriorate; and Variety lost one of its most colourful illusionists.

AN ORIENTAL veneer added a dimension of mystery to many acts. Magicians toured the East, performing tricks, picking up new ideas and learning about the great magical traditions of India and China. They were dedicated, serious students, received with respect by local conjurors who were equally delighted to expand their own repertoire by exchanging secrets. As a result, some of the great stage tricks were based on illusions practised for centuries in Eastern countries where, despite Western influences, magic is still very much a part of everyday life. While eating in a restaurant in Hong Kong's New Territories I saw a street magician enter the doorway with a forward roll and produce a bowl of goldfish from the folds of his cloak.

Howard Thurston, along with fellow Western magicians Charles Bertram and Harry Kellar travelled widely in the East looking for new material. It was a long and difficult journey in Edwardian times, with few of the basic facilities they were used to; but there was another reason for enduring the discomfort. Each of them wanted, perhaps above anything, to return with the legendary Indian Rope Trick, but none were successful. There are many well-documented accounts of it, reaching back 600 years, but the illusion is now reliably regarded as one of the great travellers' tales and an indisputable myth.

As early as 1355, Ibn Batuta, a North African Arab traveller, claimed to have seen it performed at the summer palace in

The Indian Rope Trick as performed by Fakir Carem Dumbila, impersonated here by Horace Goldin, the only white man in the world to discover the secret.

Hangchau, China. The magician tossed a leather thong into the air, where it remained upright, and a small boy climbed up hand over hand until he vanished. The shock of the illusion, watched after a heavy meal, almost gave Batuta a heart attack. His accounts are as convincing as those written hundreds of years later by nineteenth-century travellers to India but, despite their similarities, no one could provide evidence of seeing it performed.

Bertram stayed six months in India, earning himself the title Shaitan Wallah – approximately, an emissary of the devil – as he demonstrated his own tricks and studied the illusions of 176 conjurors around the country. He returned unimpressed: 'I have no hesitation in saying,' he told reporters awaiting his return at the dockside, 'that there is not a single trick which the Indians perform that European conjurors cannot do as well, and even better.'

'And what about the rope trick?' they asked.

'Moonshine!' Bertram snorted. 'There is no such trick. During my tour I asked for that trick, and not a single soul did I find who could do that, or had ever seen it. I heard of men who had heard of others who had seen it, but I could get no direct evidence. I shall try again to find someone who can do that trick for me – or the related one of throwing a chain on which a goat, a dog and finally a man climb – but until I have seen it with my own eyes I adhere to my opinion – moonshine!'

Bertram's views were confirmed years later in 1934 when the Magic Circle offered 500 guineas to anyone who could perform the rope trick. *The Times of India*, sensing a story, added 10,000 rupees of its own money, but there were still no takers. Variety magicians, nevertheless, attempted their own versions, together with Westernized variations of Indian tricks picked up on their travels. Bertram revealed the secrets of some of them to *Strand* magazine, and it is interesting to see how the illusions he witnessed eighty years ago in palace courtyards and dusty market squares still surface in cabaret today.

'I witnessed the basket trick,' he wrote, 'in which a boy disappears. The basket is peculiarly shaped, being much larger at the bottom than it is at the top. The lid is perhaps 30 inches by 18 inches, and is oval, while the basket itself spreads out to 4 ft 6 ins. This is shown empty to the audience, and a man or boy – who invariably wears a turban and some striking article of clothing – is brought forward by the conjuror. He is then put into the basket and crouches down, doing everything to emphasize the fact that it is only just large enough for him, a fact insisted on later by the lid not being allowed to fit closely.

'Now the conjuror takes a large piece of thick cloth or blanket, six feet square, and covers the basket entirely. The boy is, of course, in the basket now. The moment he gets in he has taken off his turban and any little article of clothing he can spare – for example, the brightly coloured jacket. Then he lies at the bottom of the basket and curls round it eelwise. The performer removes the cloth and drives a sword through the front of the basket, and then through the top to the bottom. Of course, he takes good care to miss the boy, as he does when he next drives the weapon through the back, high up and diagonally to the front.

'Meantime, the boy wriggles round from one side to the other, the basket being held down by other men in order to prevent it moving. The business with the sword is repeated several times so that it seems to go through every part of the basket.

'The cloth is now put over the basket again and the conjuror, placing his hand under it, removes the lid, takes out the turban and the jacket, and throws them away. Then, as if enraged at some remark which is made by one of his comrades, he

'He jumps into the basket.'

'Snatches in the air with the blanket as if catching a body.'

jumps into the basket, but as the cloth covers it, it is impossible for any member of the audience to see inside it. The people believe that it is empty while, of course, the boy remains curled up along one side.

'The conjuror now gets out of the basket, leaving the cloth over it, and puts the lid back under it. Suddenly he darts forward and snatches in the air with the blanket, as if catching a body, and goes back with much jabbering and excitement to the basket. He covers it with the blanket and something is seen moving under the cloth. Immediately the lid of the basket goes up. In another moment the boy makes his smiling reappearance.'

Mundane though the explanation seems, the trick itself, when skilfully performed, was quite baffling. Bertram went on to describe the secrets of two more illusions

which have since been duplicated in various forms. As the Magic Circle plays its cards close to its chest his article, written in December 1899, gives a rare insight into the nuts and bolts of the magician's method.

'I also witnessed the mango-tree trick, which consists in planting a seed, and showing the plant when it has grown to a certain height, and later on when it has grown still more and borne fruit. Now there is nothing simpler than the way in which these tricks are done, as you will agree when I have explained them step by step. The performer first picks a piece of mango tree about six inches high, with a tuft of three or four little leaves. This is pushed up inside the little rag doll, which is hollow in the middle, and which is always used by the Indian conjuror instead of the magic wand of the European. He then gets a large piece of the tree, about eighteen inches high, to which is attached by artificial means a little green mango. This branch he wraps tightly in a large piece of wet cloth to be used at the proper time. He also provides himself with two mango seeds, one of which is perfectly normal, and the other as like it as possible in size. This latter he slits in the centre and puts in a little wedge of wood to hold it open. At the other side he affixes three or four little bits of string, and he pares down the end of the branches so that they fit inside the slit in the prepared seed.

'Having made all his arrangements, the conjuror advances with four little bamboo sticks, tied round the top with a piece of string, after having handed them round for inspection. Round these he puts a piece of thin material, which hangs over the top and covers the front and two sides loosely, but not the back, thus forming a sort of tent which is open behind. This tent is about three feet high and the thinness of the cloth allows the interior to be seen dimly through.

'The juggler next gets a tin pot, which is

filled with mud and handed round for inspection. On the earth he pours the water, and as soon as the audience is satisfied that the pot contains nothing but mud, he hands round the first seed and asks someone to push it into the wet earth. He then puts the pot into the tent and lets the cloth drop over it. Suddenly he appears to

'He then comes to the front of the tent and lifts up the cloth.'

notice that the audience can see through the cloth, so he takes a large piece of thick cloth, in a fold of which is hidden the mango branch, and covers the thin cloth with it. When he lifts both cloths together you can see the pot is still there and unchanged.

'He now procures a chatty, or pot, of water and sprinkles it with his hand into the tent to water the seed. Here the first part of the trick ends – for the seed is supposed to take some time to germinate – and the conjuror begins doing other tricks in front of the tent. When he has finished he goes behind the tent, taking his mystic rag doll, in which there is more than meets the eye, with him. Under cover of the tent, squatting on his haunches, he pulls out of the doll the first little sprig of mango with the three or four leaves on it, and inserts the end into the slit in the mango seed. He then takes out the original seed from the pot, stuffing the other one into its place. Then he lifts up the curtain from the front, waters the pot again and takes it out to show the audience which is astonished to

see that the original seed has grown up in so short a time. He even takes the old plant out of the pot to show the bits of string, now covered in mud, which look like little roots. When he replants the seed he pretends to re-water the plant, giving himself the opportunity to take out the big piece of plant from the cloth.'

After another suitable interval for tricks, the plant is produced fully grown. Charles Bertram used a variation of the illusion in

'The original seed has grown up.'

'He pretends to water the plant.'

'He finds to his own amazement that the tree has grown.'

his stage act in which a rose tree grew, and produced blooms for the audience. It was one of many he revamped for Edwardian variety-goers; in another, so popular that another magician based a whole act around it, he produced any drink on request:

'The Indian conjuror drinks a chatty of water into which a lot of powdered chalks have been sprinkled. He then asks what colour you would like him to bring. According to the word he blows on to a white plate the required tint. For this trick all the colours are merely wrapped up separately in a small quantity of skin, like goldbeater's skin, and secreted under the lips. Of course, as soon as each little packet has been broken it is quite easy to swallow the skin. Conjurors, I may tell you, often swallow more things than they care to digest.

'I myself perform a modification of this trick, but in a much more intricate manner, and certainly no-one has yet been able to discover how it is done. I take an ordinary decanter and glass, wash them in sight of the audience, and fill the decanter with water. Then I pour port, sherry, absinthe, whiskey and milk from it in turn at the desire of anyone in the audience. Then I wash the glass and decanter again and repeat the trick, which I finish by producing champagne – the goodness of which I attest by drinking it myself. . .'

Tricks like that ensured that variety magicians were regarded with awe both off-stage and on. Once recognized in public, crowds would gather asking them to perform, and an inbuilt sense of showmanship and publicity could not allow them to refuse. Close-range tricks are, if anything, easier to perform for the skilled conjuror, because the observer's breadth and angle of vision is more restricted. On stage they specialized in the grand illusion, but while sets were being changed and props shifted, it was necessary to have a repertoire of sleight-of-hand to perform in front of tabs to keep the audience amused.

Actor John Castle, who plays magician Ganga Dun in *Lost Empires*, spent hours learning the Chinese linking rings trick, which requires a high degree of dexterity. His teacher, magical advisor David Hemingway, critcially watched the take

Nick Ollanton (played by John Castle) practising with Chinese rings.

and pronounced John up to Magic Circle standards. It was exactly the sort of stunt that audiences of 1913 would have enjoyed. Variety magicians were old hands at close-up work with cards, coins and billiard balls, but even the best-rehearsed party pieces could have unexpected results. . .

Magician Alexander Herrmann invited a guest to dinner at his hotel and could not resist trying to impress him. When a lettuce heart was served, he leaned across the table, ruffled the leaves and took an

John Castle learns from his magical adviser, David Hemingway.

expensive ring from among them, asking casually: 'Pardon me, is this yours?' Unfortunately he had picked on the wrong man. 'Yes indeed,' said his guest, humorist Bill Nye, 'I frequently leave valuables in strange places – but I have no use for it,' and he promptly presented it to the waitress. Herrmann, considerably paler, had a difficult job persuading her to return it.

Howard Thurston had a similarly uncomfortable experience travelling from Butte City to Denver. When the train stopped to take on water he passed the time performing sleight-of-hand tricks for a group of local Indians. As the departure bell rang, and the train prepared to leave, he wrapped up his impromptu show by 'finding' three twenty-dollar gold pieces in one of the Indian's pockets. The delighted man immediately claimed the money. When Thurston protested, the chief stepped forward and over-ruled him, decreeing that the money belonged to the Indian.

FEW VARIETY magicians could get by solely on sleight-of-hand. The vastness of Edwardian theatres and audience's tastes for dazzling spectacle called for the grand illusion, achieved by a maze of hidden ropes, pulleys, trap-doors, wires and mirrors. David Hemingway faced a difficult task recreating Priestley's original tricks from the novel. To give director Alan Grint freedom to work without camera tricks, every illusion had to function just as it would have done before World War I. Props, such as tables, couches and chairs were all ponderously heavy items, built to withstand knocks in transit. Big-name stage magicians toured with their own carpenters, painters and mechanics who carried out on-the-spot repairs when equipment was damaged. They travelled with the props in spacious private railway vans, accompanied by trunks of tools, paint tins and raw materials – everything to make the show completely self-sufficient.

One of Ganga Dun's popular illusions, which Priestley had seen performed by several variety acts, was the Magic Garden – an empty stage which sprang to life with trees, flowers, birds and fountains, building into a colourful spectacle. The illusion was also an old panto favourite in which grottoes and woodland scenes could be produced through removable boards and intricate traps, enabling actors and props to be propelled at great speed from the bowels of the stage with the aid of pulleys and bags of sand as counterweights.

The Grand Theatre of Varieties in Stoke, where Mr Marsden met the vanishing lady, had twenty-five trap-doors, causing powerful air currents to howl beneath the stage and snatch the sheet music from orchestra stands. Working class audiences saw little straight theatre, apart from small touring companies who played on their love of gimmickry by incorporating stage tricks at every opportunity. When Fred Hood's Stock Company visited Stoke with a selection of blood-tub melodramas Mr Marsden's son Frank witnessed an unexpected audience reaction. A cry ran round the stalls warning the hero that the villain was stalking him with a collapsible stage knife, when a man ran from the audience in a state of great excitement and stabbed the unfortunate actor.

The art of manipulating audiences is the magician's stock in trade. In the heyday of Variety they were masters of the theory that magic is nine tenths distraction, and used a thorough understanding of human psychology to make an illusion work. Fred Kelly, a friend of John Mulholland, who was an outstanding magician, became privy to some of his secrets of how to handle audiences. Mulholland always preferred an intelligent audience because he believed that people with logical, well-trained minds were not suspicious of natural movements. They were so intent on linking them into a rational chain that they could easily be deceived.

'They try to explain what they see according to their wide knowledge of cause and effect,' he said. 'If a sequence of movements seems logical to them, they fail to observe the deception from which it distracts their attention. Children, lacking adult knowledge and habits of inference, rely on direct observation. Point your finger at something across the room and an adult looks in the direction you indicate, but the child looks first at your finger. That is why a magician, when asking for a volunteer from the audience, tries to pick a

Ganga Dun
performing the
Magic Garden trick.

high-brow type rather than a moron who would use his eyes instead of his mind.

'Mulholland picks out his man and asks: "May I look at your hand?" Nobody could refuse so modest a request, and the man holds up his hand. "Ah," exclaims Mulholland, as if he has discovered something rare, "that's admirable! Won't you please hold it up for everyone to see?" Then, as if an afterthought: "Bring it right up here." By that time the man has already become conspicious and it is easier to do as he is told than to balk.

'Mulholland does not saunter onto the stage but enters at a brisk walk and stops at a certain spot; thus the audience quickly receives an impression of a man who knows what he is about. The magician must make the audience like him. For this, modesty is helpful. One of Mulholland's tricks is to make a cage with a bird in it disappear. "When I throw this cage in the air," he announces, "it will completely vanish" – and then he adds, "I *hope!*" Aside from the human appeal of this, the implication that conceivably the cage might not vanish only adds to the expectancy.'

Even the best psychology is no match for an assistant on an off-night. One variety theatre, situated on a corner, had an early cinema sandwiched between the main door and the stage entrance. The magician's assistant, taking part in a vanishing act, was plummeted through a concealed trap and had to run out of the stage door and enter the back of the auditorium to make a spectacular entrance firing a pistol. Unfortunately it was the opening night in a new town and he took the wrong turning. Cinema patrons watching a jerky silent western were startled to see a man in strange costume charge down the aisle discharging a revolver.

Reliable, imaginative craftsmen played an essential role in the touring magician's entourage. On the road the act had to be constantly improved and developed; new tricks were often constructed on tour and

tested when the theatre was empty. Big-name illusionists felt tremendous competitive pressure to create tricks more dramatic and more mystifying than their rivals. They were often inventors and engineers in their own right – square pegs who were drawn to magic because no nine-to-five career could provide a satisfying outlet for their creative energy.

Milbourne Christopher, an American illusionist has built up a collection of private papers and diaries of the great variety magicians which reveal their ingenuity. 'Magicians have been called the scientists of showbusiness,' he says. 'Robert-Houdin designed the world's first electrically-controlled protection system and installed it on his estate at St Gervais, near Blois, in France. When the master clock struck midnight, burglar alarms were activated. Should a prowler attempt to force open a window or door, a warning bell immediately sounded. Another automatic timing device set off three wake-up signals at different times in different areas. This also tripped the suspended container in the barn which delivered morning oats to his horse.

'When a visitor rapped the knocker on the post by the gates of the winding road that led to the magician's house, a bell sounded in the hallway. Fifteen years before Thomas A. Edison perfected his incandescent lamp, Robert-Houdin installed a battery-powered circuit to illuminate the château on the occasion of his daughter's first communion.

'Earlier performers – Garnerin, Pinetti and Oehler – made balloon ascensions. Gernerin is credited with inventing the first practical parachute. John Nevil Maskelyne, founder of the British conjuring dynasty, devised a ribbonless typewriter with ninety-six characters, and patented and sold coin-operated locks for public doors and coin-activated vending machines. Houdini designed the mutli-drawer theatrical trunk, was a pioneer aviator and made the first successful flight in Australia. Georges Melies introduced movie camera techniques still in use today. . .'

IN THE rococo world of Variety, where talent was mixed, personalities often tormented and private lives frequently disastrous, magicians were stern taskmasters but, because the discipline of their work, tended to be stable, reasonable individuals. Supervising a complex show where anything could go wrong, and wrestling with the logistics of shifting tons of equipment from theatre to theatre, made them accomplished administrators and accountants, too. Like Priestley's Ganga Dun, they provided a livelihood for large numbers of people. It was a mutual benefit society – magicians could not survive without their helpers' skills, and the crew had no other means of earning such a lucrative living.

The Great Lafayette, a brilliantly inventive German illusionist born Sigmund Neuberger, made heroic attempts to save the lives of his company and animals when fire engulfed an Edinburgh theatre during a performance in 1911. Neuberger was brought up in America where, after successfully launching himself on the Vaudeville circuit with oriental illusions, he changed his name to Lafayette. He was to become the most eccentric magician in Variety, and one in whom the pressures of the profession could bring out the best and worst extremes. Lafayette was adored by the public and hated by his employees who were drilled every day, military fashion.

An early show business journalist who eavesdropped on a backstage roll-call heard Lafayette bellow to a line of staff: 'From the right – number! One . . . two . . . three . . . four . . . stop! You Cecile, shout more clearly. And you Alice, throw your shoulders back. Don't forget – you're assistants of the greatest magician in the world!'

If any of his team had the misfortune to meet him off duty – and they avoided him strenuously – they were under instructions to spring smartly to attention and give a full military salute. 'That is their duty,' the illusionist would say. 'They are privates in the Great Lafayette's army.' They loathed him, but rarely left because he paid bigger wages than any magician on the road. Lafayette could afford to, because he was almost solely responsible for putting illusionists into a high income bracket. He was a tough negotiator with theatre management, and never accepted less than £300. In return he always fulfilled his promise to play to packed houses. When he arrived in England he demanded £1,500 for a two-week run at a London music hall, a request which the management understandably turned down. Lafayette responded by hiring the theatre himself for an agreed fee, ending his run a fortnight later with a clear profit of more than £1,500. 'Which,' he remarked to the house manager, 'just shows what I'm worth and what the public thinks of me.'

In the eyes of ordinary people he was a hero who could do no wrong. Shortly before leaving for Britain he invited a woman out to dinner at a Chicago restaurant. 'The lady's husband quite by chance strolled in and asked Lafayette what the blazes he meant,' reported *Everybody's Weekly*. 'Lafayette stood up and hit the unfortunate man on the chin. When the fellow recovered, the manager of the restaurant threatened him with a summons for assaulting such an illustrious client as the Great Lafayette.'

Lafayette's illusions were highly original and lived up to his motto: 'Let it be spectacular!' One of his favourite bookings was the London Hippodrome, where everyone knew that there were no stage trap-doors. It added to the element of mystery, making his deceptively simple tricks seem even more baffling. In one of the most popular of them, Lafayette would walk on in flowing Chinese robes and

Lafayette's Chinese trick using a dog.

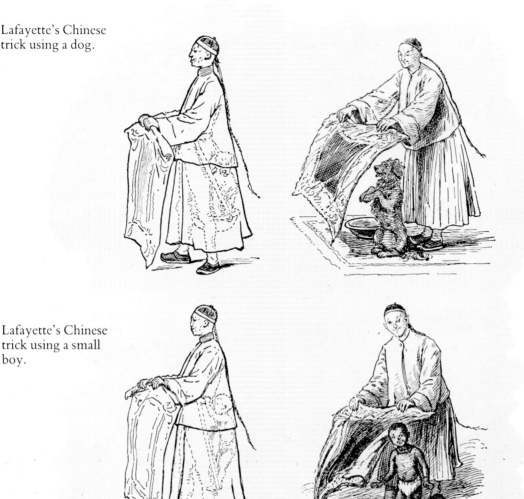

Lafayette's Chinese trick using a small boy.

shake a large square of silk from his sleeve. He held it by the corners, allowing it to float to the floor, then snatched it away to reveal a large teddy bear which came to life and waddled into the wings.

The secret of this ingenious trick was a tiny folding seat attached to a broad leather belt around his waist beneath his robes. A small child dressed in a teddy bear outfit dropped from the perch at the critical moment while Lafayette, with great dexterity, gave the impression that the bear was rising from the ground. At Hanley, in the Potteries, the illusion came to an end when magistrates fined him for employing

child labour. Lafayette's manager, Leon de Valois, immediately dispatched two dwarves on the next train north as substitutes.

His act was the epitome of Edwardian magic, crystallizing everything pre-war audiences loved to see. In one typical set the curtains opened on a sculptor's studio with Lafayette, in artist's smock, working on a large clay model of Leda and the Swan. As the clay took shape it suddenly came to life, surrounded by fountains lit with electric lights which made the water change colour. Tricks involving artist's canvasses were also highly popular –

Priestley's characters in *Lost Empires* used a painting illusion – and Lafayette created one of the finest. In the setting of an artist's garret he was seen putting the finishing touches to a portrait of the Tsar which stepped out of the frame on to the stage. At the same moment Lafayette walked off into the wings – and the moment he disappeared from view the Tsar removed his false beard and Royal hat to reveal the magician himself.

Lafayette was not particularly liked by his fellow magicians, and did not spend much time in their company. To add to the ill-feeling no one could top his bombastic finale when he rode on stage in full military uniform, astride a prancing white horse, escorted by a mounted band of twenty musicians, to the sound of a twenty-one gun salute and waving flags. Follow that, as they say.

The master of 'conjuration and mighty magic' was a bachelor who loved the company of attractive women. His greatest weakness and constant indulgence, however, was not the attention of his lady followers, but his dog Beauty. Lafayette doted on the white crossbred hound to the point of fixing a brass plaque outside his London home bearing an engraving of Beauty and the inscription: 'The more I see of men, the more I love my dog.'

The Great Lafayette with his dog.

His devotion was total – Beauty's portrait appeared on all Lafayette's Credit Lyonnais cheques and theatrical contracts. He had three other dogs, but only Beauty became the object of his obsessive affection. She cost £20 a week to keep – almost enough to feed a working family for a month – dining on four-course dinners, complete from soup to pudding. And when Beauty went walkies it was only with a diamond encrusted gold collar, matching bracelets on her legs and a solid silver walking chain.

Outside the magician's suffocatingly plush home, medallions of Beauty were embedded in the walls between overstuffed window boxes. Inside, the dog had its own bathroom, a gold bed hung with mauve swags and drapes, and its own special seat in the illusionist's mauve Mercedes. On the bonnet there was, naturally, a mascot of Beauty rampant grasping the Stars and Stripes.

His life revolved around the dog, and when it died in 1911, in his suite at the Caledonian Hotel, Edinburgh, Lafayette reached the point of breakdown. At first he refused to go on stage that night, but the manager talked him into it; he walked from the wings sobbing uncontrollably with tears rolling down his face. Beauty, meanwhile, lay in state on a mauve silk cushion, swathed in banks of lilies. Lafayette commissioned an £800 mausoleum in the city's Piershill Cemetery, but immediately ran into problems with local Presbyterian authorities who refused to bury a dog on consecrated ground – even if it did have its own oak coffin. A compromise was quickly reached when Lafayette signed a document to say that the vault would also be his own resting place. As he signed the paper with his usual flourish, the magician could scarcely have imagined that in little more than a week he would be joining her.

The night before Beauty's lavish funeral, Lafayette again had to be talked into going on-stage at the Empire theatre in Nichol-son Street. Its copper dome and gilt plasterwork had been specially commissioned by Moss Empires, whose brief to architect Frank Matcham was to build the most beautiful theatre in Scotland. The interior of white, gold and pale green, with red velvet seating and classical statues, was one of his finest achievements. Moss Empires were so delighted that they intended it to be chosen for the 1912 Royal Variety Performance, but it was never to be.

Lafayette and members of his forty-strong company were acknowledging the applause for their illusion, The Lion's Bride, on a set lavishly decorated as a harem. The spot always drew an enthusiastic reception – a shipwrecked girl forced into marrying an Arab prince has the choice of succumbing to his unwelcome advances, or walking into a lion's cage. She nobly chooses the latter and, as the lion springs it transforms in mid-air into her lover – the Great Lafayette, naturally. The effect was achieved by a concealed revolving door which substituted Lafayette, and swept the lion into a concealed cage, while his assistants momentarily stepped forward to block the audience's view.

The magician, incidentally, had suffered a mixed relationship with Arizona, the ill-tempered lion which had toured with him for years. The man who cossetted Beauty had been fined for cruelty to animals in Pittsburgh, when he admitted making the beast roar by passing an electric current through a metal plate in the floor of its cage. Arizona, understandably touchy, had retaliated on two occasions, mauling him badly.

As the company stepped forward for its final bow a huge oriental lantern above them short-circuited and spluttered until a tiny tongue of flame licked up its framework and touched the bottom of a canvas backdrop in the flies above. The stage manager spotted the first warning puff of smoke creeping beneath the proscenium arch, and yanked the safety curtain lever. The curtain jammed a yard from the stage floor, and the audience were unaware of the pandemonium backstage until the orchestra leader had the presence of mind to strike up the national anthem. The packed house incredibly managed to clear the building in three minutes, but the breeze from the exit doors suddenly lifted the flames, causing the blazing oriental lantern to crash to the stage. One of Lafayette's assistants tried to drag the light clear of the props as blazing scenery plunged on to the heads of the cast and stage-hands.

The jealous secrecy with which Lafayette guarded his act had imprisoned them in an inferno of nightmare proportions. He always insisted that the pass door, leading from the stage to the auditorium, was locked to prevent people creeping from the stalls to see how his illusions worked. It meant that the company were effectively trapped on stage, with their only escape blocked by a crazed Arizona, who had battered his way out of the cage with his mane on fire. By the time firemen arrived the safety curtain had buckled in the intense heat and crashed onto the stage, dragging masonry with it. Ten people burned to death, and an eleventh died later in hospital from severe burns.

Lafayette had played his last show, but not his final illusion. His body, wearing the silver sword he carried for the lion act, was found near Arizona's cage where he had fallen, presumably trying to save the animal. The corpse was taken to the morgue and prepared for cremation while the head count of the dead continued; but back in the ruins of the Empire, only nine of the missing ten people could be accounted for. Three days later a workman clearing the rubble found an expensive ring, which he took to Alfred Nisbet, Lafayette's solicitor. They returned to search the debris and found a body lying face down. The man wearing the silver sword who had been cremated was Frank Richards, who doubled for Lafayette in the illusion. Edinburgh University's Professor of Medical Jurisprudence established that the last body to be recovered was that of the magician. He was buried next to Beauty at a funeral attended by all the leading theatrical celebrities of the day, including Houdini, who had given Lafayette the dog twelve years earlier at Nashville Opera House.

THE KING AND QUEEN were unable to enjoy the magnificence of the Edinburgh Empire for the Royal Command Performance, but this did not diminish their interest in magic. Like their subjects they were fascinated by it. Today, when people readily accept all the wonders of the age, from the space shuttle to computer graphics, there is still a deep urge to discover the secrets of stage illusionists' tricks. How the lady vanishes, or the mystery of rabbits produced from hats intrigue audiences who may not show the slightest curiosity in fibre optics or facsimile transmission machines. Royalty, who might be expected to be above such things, have shown an equally keen interest; in the heyday of Variety many famous magicians were called to give private shows in the Royal houses.

Variety illusionist Douglas Beaufort was sent by Edward VII on a diplomatic mission to Morocco where the king, who had fallen under the disturbing influence of his court magicians, was treated to a demonstration of superior British magic. Beaufort produced eggs from the senior interpreter's mouth, and yards of ribbon from the King of Morocco's own dagger. As a result, the court magicans were made redundant and Beaufort was appointed his official advisor. The Shah of Persia, on a state visit to London, was equally delighted with a private performance of Beaufort's card tricks and ventriloquism. When it ended he was visibly disappointed at having to sit through a film of Queen Victoria's jubilee.

Public faith in magicians' skills was such that Beaufort found himself invited, at the turn of the century, to put on a show at the home of a West Country Duchess. As soon as he arrived he was ushered into her ladyship's private apartment and told: 'I have a peculiar commission for you after the show tonight. If you perform it well you will receive a fee of 100 guineas.' Beaufort, a little perplexed, listened as the Duchess explained that she wished him to impersonate the ghost of a woman who had been locked in the east wing centuries earlier, and had died of thirst. 'You are to hide in a room I shall show you, and when you hear two people meet there, you are to make the noise of a door being nailed up, and some screams. You are to make them thoroughly terrified.'

Beaufort, who could not resist asking who the couple were, was told that it was the Duke and his lover, an actress who happened to be a weekend house guest. His hammerings and screams were so effective that, a few days later, a cheque arrived for double the promised amount, with a note: 'The Duchess was much pleased with your performance, which she thought most amusing and effective.'

Beaufort never revealed her identity – an uncharacteristic gesture, as variety artists were less than discreet in publicizing their links with the aristocracy. The undignified scramble by artists advertising that they had appeared at the Royal Command Performance in 1912 was equalled only by that of Dr J. W. Holden, who was summoned by Queen Victoria to give a conjuring demonstration at Balmoral. His delivery, a blend of bravado and bare-faced cheek, was surprisingly well received by the Queen. Even the dour John Brown, her close friend, was not offended when asked to select a card. 'I hope you don't imagine Mr Brown to be a confederate of mine,' Holden announced. 'You can always,

your Majesty, tell a confederate by his sinister looks, and I am sure there is nothing of that about Mr Brown's honest face. . .'

The show, which had a few moments of inspired magic between a surfeit of simple card tricks, was greatly enjoyed by the Royal party. Holden left immediately to order garish posters trumpeting: 'Dr Holden, the Queen's Magician, has the honour to announce that he is prepared to repeat, either in private or in public, the Marvellous Entertainment entitled CHARMATION, as given by him at Balmoral Castle before Her Most Gracious Majesty THE QUEEN-EMPRESS, who personally complimented him on his success.'

PUBLICITY, the louder the better, was an integral part of Edwardian showmanship, and few mastered the art as skilfully as Harry Houdini. Bill posters for his first London appearance at the Alhambra boldly quoted *The Times*, with the rather cryptic line: 'Locks, bolts and bars fly asunder.' Houdini, 'The Marvel of the Age, The Wizard of the Chains, The Demon of the Cells, The Mystic of the World,' was among a handful of magicians who could justifiably boast of his exploits; many of his tricks were unique and have never been repeated. Houdini's name – which honoured his great idol Robert-Houdin – was so synonymous with escapology that it passed into English usage.

His arrival in London was billed as The Modern Jack Sheppard, a reference to an eighteenth-century Spitalfields carpenter who turned to crime. It was praise indeed – by 1900 there was a long list of books about Sheppard's exploits. His first escape from custody was through a hole in the roof of St Giles' roundhouse. Then, caught picking pockets, he was locked in Newgate Ward, New Prison, where he filed through his chains, cut the bars from the window and dropped 8 m (25 ft) to the ground on

The performer fastened with six pairs of handcuffs.

The handkerchief and key drawn from the waistcoat.

knotted sheets.

Sheppard was sentenced to death at the Old Bailey in 1724, but made a sensational escape from the death cell at Newgate Prison by finding a narrow ventilation passage which led to a warder's cottage. Sheppard was recaptured raiding a Fleet Street watchmaker's shop and returned to Newgate. In the prison's strongest cell he was handcuffed and shackled to 136 kg (300 lb) of assorted ironmongery (the authorities were clearly taking no chances) and chained to the middle of the floor. Remarkably he found a tiny nail in a crack between the flagstones and picked the lock on his tethering chain. His fetters, however, had been fitted by a blacksmith without locks. He broke them all by searching for the weakest links and using brute force. Sheppard escaped up a chimney, but 2 m (6 ft) up encountered an iron bar, which he patiently removed by picking away the mortar with a broken chain link.

'He climbed on and came out in a room above,' according to one account, 'a room that had been locked for at least seven

Unlocking the handcuffs with the key.

years. There he found another nail and, using that and his chimney bar, he forced off the door lock and let himself into a passage. Another door faced him, bolted on the far side. With his bar he pierced the door and drew the bolt – all this without disturbing a single warder. Soon he found himself in the prison chapel, and reached the loft through a trapdoor in the ceiling.

Here he forced two more doors and reached the prison roof at about eight pm.'

After six hours gruelling labour Sheppard found that the nearest adjoining roof was too far away for a safe jump. Incredibly, he returned to his cell for a blanket and lowered himself down. After 150 years of reading and re-reading such tales, London was ready for Harry Houdini. His reputation had preceeded him across the Atlantic, but he still had to convince the theatre manager that his act was all that he claimed before the contract could be signed. Houdini obliged by freeing himself from handcuffs at Scotland Yard. He had studied the technique for five years, buying every available type of police handcuff, dismantling it and fashioning lock-picks which could be concealed on his body.

Word of the Scotland Yard escape quickly spread, and 2,000 people jammed the opening night at the Alhambra. On his successful European tour which followed, Houdini appeared in Moscow, where he was intrigued by the horse-drawn prison vans used to transport detainees to Siberian labour camps. They were reinforced, and without windows, save for a small grille in the door at the back. The authorities considered them so escape-proof, that when he challenged the Chief of Secret Police that he could break out of one, he was given permission to try.

Houdini managed to manoeuvre the van so that its single rear door was backed against a courtyard wall to protect his secrets. A team of undercover policemen stripped him, chained him hand and foot, and bundled him inside, padlocking the door. Twenty minutes later he was walking across the cobbled yard politely asking for his clothes. The embarrassed authorities hushed up the incident for fear of losing face, and Houdini later revealed his method. He had noticed one weak link in the prison van's security – the door grille was just within reach of the padlock, which could be easily unpicked.

Houdini's escapes in those unhurried pre-World War I days give an interesting illustration of how the pace of life has changed. Some of his more complex stunts took up to an hour, even ninety minutes, but audiences were prepared to wait in tense silence to see if he could free himself. Today, when a five-minute television spot is considered an eternity, it is difficult to believe that audiences possessed such reserves of uncomplaining patience. Of course, the longer the routine, the more frequently Houdini would momentarily emerge from behind his screen – still chained – or from within his curtained cabinet, to maintain contact with them. The importance of this was bitterly brought home to him when he devised his first escape from a straight-jacket. A doctor friend obtained a canvas restraining garment from a mental hospital, and Houdini spent hours rolling on the floor, using all his strength to slip an arm over his head, and open the stiff buckles through the thick fabric. When he finally mastered the technique, a feat no one had previously attempted let alone accomplished, he performed it on stage behind a curtain. He emerged triumphantly holding the jacket above his head to be greeted by an absence of applause – everyone thought that a stage-hand had untied him when he was out of view. After that Houdini tried to make his escapes as visible as possible, hiding his secret techniques only when necessary.

Like many variety artists he was pressured by public taste to attempt more and more bizarre escapes and, as a consummate showman, he was happy to oblige. The only trick he preferred not to repeat was an occasion when, manacled and chained, he was stuffed head-first into the carcase of a whale-like creature which had been washed up on a beach, and carted away as a side-show. The slit in the creature's body was stitched up with chain and the crowd waited. Houdini's manacles were not particularly complicated, but it took him a

Poster advertising Houdini's death-defying mystery.

quarter of an hour to escape – on several occasions he almost lapsed into unconsciousness, overcome by embalming fluid which had been tossed by the bucketful into the 'sea monster's' stomach.

Houdini's most celebrated trick was the Chinese Water Torture, in which he was handcuffed and lowered head down into a narrow tank of water with his feet clamped to a heavy wooden lid. He could be seen through a plate glass window in the wall of the tank as the lid was padlocked into position. Curtains were swept round the contraption as Houdini's assistants formed a circle with raised fire axes, ready to smash the glass if he failed to escape. It seldom took him more than two minutes to free himself, and the trick became so popular that he closed his act with it from 1912.

The man who escaped from milk churns, locked trunks and crates, was thrown manacled from bridges and submerged in rivers, died as the result of a foolish dressing-room accident. A university student, J. Gordon Whitehead, visiting Houdini, suddenly asked in the middle of a conversation about biblical miracles, if he had trained himself to withstand punches to the stomach. The magician nodded and, before he had time to brace his muscles, Whitehead delivered four powerful short jabs to the solar plexus. Houdini went on to do his show complaining of stomach pains, but by the next day it was clear that he was suffering from peritonitis. He staggered through his final performance with a temperature of 104 and, despite an emergency appendix operation, died on 31 October 1926.

What he expected in the afterlife was unclear; Houdini, deeply sceptical about life after death, spent most of his career fighting spiritualism and exposing fake mediums. He offered publicly to duplicate any seance phenomena, such as flying trumpets, floating tables and rapping doors and frequently took time off from his variety career to pursue his passionate crusade. His convictions were sincere, but he was also tapping a lucrative vein of publicity material. Spiritualism made headlines in the pre-war years and prominent coverage was always given to Houdini's sensational exposés. When the *Scientific American* offered $2,500 to anyone who could create psychic phenomena under laboratory conditions, he was appointed the magazine's official investigator, and zealously ensured that no one claimed it.

The most competent fraudulent medium he encountered was Mina Crandon, 26 years old, blonde and very beautiful. Known in spiritualist circles as Margery, she had developed a gymnastic ability to contort her body in a darkened seance room and manipulate furniture, ring hidden bells and produce rapping sounds. Unfortunately Margery's illusions, for they were nothing more, strayed too close to Houdini's own territory for her to operate undetected, and her tricks were rapidly uncovered.

Houdini reproduced 'psychic phenomena' in his stage act, often terrifying impressionable members of the audience before he could explain that it was only trickery. While he worked honestly, never losing an opportunity to denounce spiritualism, other magicians masqueraded as mystics and claimed to summon up spirits on stage. It was, as they say, all done with mirrors, but naïve Edwardian theatregoers saw it as an awesome demonstration of hidden power.

JOHN MASKELYNE, the son of a Cheltenham saddler, was a veteran at spiritual hocus pocus, and made his first break into show business exposing fake mediums. By chance, two American travelling mediums, the Davenport Brothers, were appearing at Cheltenham Town Hall where, strapped inside a wooden cabinet, they made bells ring and caused musical instruments to play. The pair had been a sensation in London, where gullible audiences were convinced that they had psychic abilities. Maskelyne, sitting at the end of the front row in the darkened town hall, saw one of them through a gap in the cabinet door free his hands and pick up a bell. The young magician, who had previously only dabbled in conjuring tricks, stood up and tried to denounce them, but was shouted down by the audience. Maskelyne, smarting with indignation, decided to build a duplicate of their cabinet and publicly prove his point. With the help of his friend George Cooke, an army trumpeter, it took almost three months. They carried out a successful demonstration and, while the Davenports faded discreetly away, the new partnership toured the provinces and even appeared before the Prince of Wales at a private party.

Maskelyne took over the old Egyptian Hall in Piccadilly, which had formerly been a museum, and turned it into a theatre of magic. His ingenuity and skill established him as the father of modern conjuring, inventing illusions which are still used today. Like Houdini, the lure of exposing mediums constantly pulled him away from his work. He issued, and received, many challenges which inevitably led to full scale public arguments and made him the most litigious magician in history. Maskelyne became a familiar figure in the law courts, attacking others, or defending actions against himself. When judgments went against him, a stubborn streak made him a most ungracious loser, though generally he had a reputation for courtesy and politeness.

Maskelyne admired the skill of other magicians, but bridled when they claimed supernatural powers. He attacked a 'mentalist', Washington Irving Bishop, who foolishly tried to publicize his mind-reading act by claiming that he could genuinely read thoughts. When the American responded by accusing him of being 'devoid of honorable instincts', he underestimated Maskelyne's litigious hair-trigger. The magician instantly sued and was awarded £10,000, which he was unfortunately unable to collect as Bishop had fled the country.

In another case, Maskelyne appeared as a prosecution witness at Bow Street Court to demonstrate how Henry Slade, an American medium, wrote 'spirit messages' on a piece of slate. The trick was apparently accomplished with a tiny piece of pencil lead lodged under his finger nail. Slade was sentenced to three months imprisonment and Maskelyne stepped up his anti-spiritualist campaign with renewed zeal. His crusade was becoming such an embarrassment to sincere believers in the afterworld that the Reverend Thomas Colley, Archdeacon of Stockton, in Warwickshire, issued him with a challenge.

The Reverend Colley, convinced of the power of the spirit world, waged £1000 (a surprisingly un-clerical gesture) that he could not reproduce phenomena witnessed at a seance in his rectory nine years earlier. The medium on this occasion had been later arrested on fraud charges, but the archdeacon's faith was undiminished. The case was complicated and drawn-out, but hinged on the Reverend Colley's belief that he had seen a 'spirit form' emerge from the medium's side, walk, talk and even eat an apple, after which the medium spat out the core.

Maskelyne proved that cleric was the innocent victim of a malicious fraud by staging a special show in 1906 – THE £1000 MYSTERY. . . THE SIDE ISSUE.

Thanks to the enthusiastic efforts of the *Daily Express* the hall was packed to the doors. Newspapers generally – and *The Times* in particular – came out in favour of Maskelyne after watching his convincing performance; but the archdeacon refused to pay up because he had not been present at the show.

Writs began to fly like grapeshot as Maskelyne took Colley to court and Colley, in turn, sued the magician for libel. The judge, Mr Justice Ridley, dutifully sat through a re-run of the performance with his jury, but concluded that the phenomena had been only reproduced in part. Judgment was awarded to the archdeacon on a technicality.

One of Maskelyne's lengthy, and most costly actions went as far as the House of Lords when one of his rather brash challenges was unexpectedly taken up by two determined young engineering clerks, Stolley and Evans. The illusionist publicly boasted that he would pay £500 to anyone who could make a 'perfect imitation' of a mystery box he had used for thirty-five years in his stage show.

Maskelyne explained its history to journalists: 'When I was a young amateur I invented a small casket in which articles borrowed from the audience were placed. The casket was then tied up by another member of the audience, and in the act of passing it from him to another, I was able to extract its contents. The casket would stand any amount of examination. From that I started to make my box. Now I will tell you something about the box which I have never told anybody, and that is that by the mechanism I am able, even though imprisoned inside the box, to have complete control over the bonds which are outside. On several occasions I have escaped from the box when fifty yards of rope have been used.'

At the first trial Stolley and Evans produced a box from which one of them escaped even when tied up and the container was placed inside a canvas bag. The jury were unable to reach a unanimous verdict, but a retrial went in their favour. Maskelyne appealed to the House of Lords, basing his defence on the fact that the pair could not possibly know the secret of the mechanism, and their efforts were not therefore a 'perfect imitation.' He lost the case and was ordered to pay the £500, plus costs. To save face he immediately bounced back with another challenge, but rather less impetuously worded. The case had dragged on for two years, but the enterprising clerks were pleased with the verdict.

'We examined Mr Maskelyne's box two or three times,' Stolley said, 'but you get no opportunity for a practical inspection during the performance. We had to take our measurements very hurriedly. When we made the box he would never look at it. In fact, we consider that throughout the whole affair Mr Maskelyne treated us with contempt – until the action started.'

Their reproduction was a remarkable achievement, as Maskelyne was one of the finest illusion inventors in the business. However, as always in the unpredictable business of magic, his success rate was not one hundred per cent. One of his tricks involved borrowing a large diamond ring from a lady in the audience, which he dropped into an envelope, sealed it and set it alight. The ring, of course, vanished. Maskelyne, who allowed his assistant Bertram to perform the trick, watched as the second part unfolded. Bertram rolled a sheet of paper into a cone, paused for a few seconds, then opened it to reveal a live dove wearing the ring on a ribbon around its neck. Normally, the bird circled the audience a few times before returning to Bertram's finger. The assistant then retrieved the ring and returned it to its owner. On this occasion the dove fluttered over the audience, then fixed its beady eye on an open ventilator high in the theatre roof, and took off to freedom. Neither the

bird nor the ring were ever seen again, and Maskelyne had to pay the distressed lady £1000 compensation.

At the outbreak of World War I he was approached by the Admiralty to help in the war at sea. During the Battle of Jutland, battleship crews operating their massive sixteen-inch guns had to work in fifteen-minute relays because they were burned by the flash-back after each shell was fired. Just at a point when the Navy was gaining supremacy over the German fleet, British gun crews found that they were unable to handle the weapons effectively.

Someone at the Admiralty recalled watching Maskelyne licking red-hot pokers and handling live coals in his act, and guessed correctly that a secret preparation was used to protect his skin. The magician supplied the formula for his cream to the War Ministry, enabling naval gunners to work for long periods close to red-hot breeches. Maskelyne was also a pioneer of high-speed photography, and was called in by the War Office to photograph shells in flight on artillery test ranges to help in the development of new weapons.

In purchasing the lease on the Egyptian Hall, and later St George's Hall – both, sadly, long gone – Maskelyne reduced the tiresome necessity to travel. The BBC took over St George's Hall in 1933 and transformed its warm, colourful interior into the functional bareness of No.10 Studio. For thirty years it had been the home of levitation, vanishing ladies, cooing doves, fakirs, dwarves and mechanical robots. The plaster, the velvet and the brass fittings were ripped out as the age of the microphone finally came to Maskelyne's.

DAVID DEVANT, Maskelyne's partner after Cooke's retirement, toured extensively but, even with a large road crew it was exhausting work. Life on the road was not without its hazards, particularly abroad. Charles Carter, an American illusionist, embarked on a world tour in 1907 to weather a train crash in Bombay and an outbreak of plague in Canton. Others suffered shipwrecks, props confiscated by curious customs officers, and assistants struck down by mysterious tropical diseases.

For every enormous magic show conducted by such master illusionists as Devant, Robert-Houdin, the Great Herrmann and Servais Le Roy, there were dozens who travelled light, manipulating coins and cards, or performing clever mind-reading acts. An Italian, Bartholomeo Bosco, who was captured by the Russians while fighting on Napoleon's side, was perhaps the first of the modern sleight-of-hand school. He escaped from brutal Cossack guards to wander Europe without assistants, heavy props, or even the obligatory wide sleeves. The Pope, hearing of his simple illusions, invited him to the Vatican where he performed for an audience of Cardinals seated on rows of gold embroidered chairs.

For his opening trick he borrowed a priceless diamond-studded watch hanging from a cardinal's cape and, laying it carefully on the marble floor, crushed it beneath his heel. The Pope was visibly angry until Bartholomeo swept away the pieces and produced the watch intact from His Holiness's robes.

He revealed the secret of this rather stunning trick on his deathbed in Dresden in 1863. The watch had been a gift to the cardinal from a prominent Rome businessman, who was so impressed by the workmanship that he ordered an inexpensive duplicate to be made. Bosco had heard the story on his travels, tracked the businessman down and bought the copy for £150, swearing him to secrecy. The illusion cost him all his savings, but the ensuing publicity guaranteed him work for the rest of his life.

It was a one-off trick tailored to the occasion. In Edwardian times, audiences never tired of seeing the same feats repeated and, in the prevailing climate of spiritualism, mind-readers were among the most popular acts who travelled light. All of them worked a complex system of codes with their partners, who roamed audiences selecting items of jewellery for identification, or words written down which the mentalist had to 'read'. David Devant and his sister were so skilled at 'mental magnetism' that Sir Oliver Lodge, an occult devotee, was convinced that they had powers 'higher than those ordinarily possessed by human beings' – despite Devant's insistence that it was all trickery. Their most successful thought-reading feat was called 'translucidation'. It is so completely mystified pre-war audiences that Devant kept the secret to himself, until 1936, when he revealed all to the *Sunday People*.

His sister sat blindfolded on stage close to the footlights, while Devant distributed blank cards among the audience, on which they had to write a message, replace the card in an envelope and seal it down marking it in any way they pleased. Another member of the audience collected the cards in a black bag, which he handed to Devant.

'When all this had been done I took the bag from him with the tips of my fingers and, carrying it at arm's length, laid it on my sister's lap. She put one of her hands inside it and waited while I explained to the audience that simply by taking an envelope out of the bag and holding it to her forehead she would be able to read the message written on the card inside.

'This she then did, each envelope being passed over the footlights as its message was read, and being found to be perfectly intact by the person who had originally marked it.

'On the face of it the feat seemed to savour of black magic, so much that one day Sir Oliver Lodge, who had seen an earlier performance, came armed with a specially sealed envelope and publicly challenged my sister to read its contents.

'The Marvellous Maharajah of Mystery, The Great Ganga Dun.'

'She read it with the rest, and he was so impressed that he at once stood up in his place in the stalls and addressed the audience. In brief, he said that there was no principle known to science by which the marvel he had just witnessed could have been accomplished, and he finally hinted that I might well be employing higher powers.

'Nevill Maskelyne and I saw him after the performance, and assured him that it was a trick pure and simple, but to our surprise he told us quite frankly that he did not believe us, and went away firmly convinced that either my sister or I was a medium of no ordinary ability.

'Before he left I told him that one day, when I had retired, I would reveal the trick I had played upon him, and perhaps he will absolve me from any dabblings in black magic when I now tell him that had the audience been able to see beneath my sister's skirt they would have seen a small trap-door in the stage immediately beneath her open, and a girl's hand emerge.

'This hand took hold of a length of speaking tube attached to my sister's dress, and connected it up with another tube that led through the trap-door and into a cabinet beneath the stage. Small earphones concealed beneath my sister's hair now enabled her to hear anything spoken into the mouthpiece end of the tube in the cabinet beneath the stage.

'Next, the mysterious hand came to rest beneath a slit in the skirt across my sister's knees, and while I was making my introductory remarks to the audience my sister calmly pushed the envelopes from her bag, through the slit and into the waiting hand beneath. They were immediately passed on to another assistant in the cabinet, where, with the aid of a very powerful electric light, the message written on the card could easily be read through the envelope.

'The moment the assistant had read the first message, he handed it back to the girl and told my sister, through the speaking tube, the message on it. Meanwhile the girl had passed the envelope up to my sister via the slit, and she, pretending to take it from the bag, held it to her forehead and announced the message.'

Mind-reading was a side-line for Devant, but others built careers around it. Julius and Agnes Zancig, billed as Two Minds With But A Single Thought, were a Danish-American act who toured with Houdini's roadshow. They followed the traditional pattern of Julius going among the audience, while Agnes remained blindfolded on stage. Their code system was so sophisticated that many were convinced that they had psychic powers. The Zancigs always insisted that it was a trick but, like Sir Oliver, there were those who wanted to believe, and were determined to. In 1906, Sir Arthur Conan Doyle, who had a passionate interest in the supernatural, insisted on writing them a testimonial: 'I have tested Professor and Mrs Zancig today, and I am quite sure that their remarkable performance as I saw it is due to psychic-based thought-transference, and not to trickery.' The Zancigs, tired of trying to convince him otherwise, used the letter as publicity material. After Agnes' death Julius settled in California where he sold $10 crystal balls complete with instructions.

Throughout their career they were made several offers for their code, but refused to sell. Good tricks were guaranteed a long life and, as magicians toured abroad more than any other performers because their material was international, some illusions were successfully 'milked' for up to half a century. They were considered a valuable asset and often sold for vast sums. More commonly, however, other illusionists acquired them by piracy, with the result that many touring magic shows had variations of each other's tricks, embroidered with a little showmanship and different stage effects.

The vanishing lady, despite being used in countless permutations, never seemed to lose its audience appeal. The most ingenious version was undoubtedly that of Dr de Buatier, who covered his lady with a large square of silk, then tossed her into the air, making both his assistant and the fabric disappear. It was one of the most highly-skilled illusions ever staged, requiring speed, perfect timing and years of practice. When the lady was seated on a chair and covered, the silk contained fine wires moulded to her outline. She then catapulted through a spring trap while Buatier picked up the outline and tossed it into the air with a flourish. The silk, through a highly complicated system of loops and pulleys concealed in his clothing, vanished up his sleeve so quickly that the audience, distracted by rapid masking movements, literally did not see it happen.

The great variety magicians were both perfectionists and originators. Their inventive minds were never still, and all their illusions were based on an impressive knowledge of human psychology, manipulating their audience as much as the silk or the cards. They were in complete control from the moment they stepped on stage, directing the audience where to look with a gesture or an outstretched hand, like kittens distracted by a ball of wool. For the brief duration of their performances they were gods, and their audiences, applauding in awe and wonder, acknowledged it. Immaculate in evening dress they took their bows and until the moment the curtain fell, the atmosphere was truly magic.

# PAINTED LADIES

*Ta-Ra-Ra-Boom-De-Ay* dance music.

WHEN MARIE LLOYD, the Queen of Comedy, died in 1922 at her home in Golders Green, three days after collapsing on stage, Londoners mourned her passing as though she were royalty. On the day of her funeral they lined the route in their tens of thousands. Barrow boys, flower girls, stage-hands, street hawkers, the old and the poor began the long trek to the cemetery at dawn because they could not afford a bus ticket. All the buses were full anyway, moving at a mournful walking pace in the heavy stream of traffic alongside the tide of humanity on the pavement. 'Nearly everyone was crying,' newspapers reported. 'For three days the crowds passed by in their last tribute. And huge bouquets left by the wealthy were nearly smothered beneath pathetic little bunches tied with string.' An estimated 120,000 people paid their last respects at the graveside.

Marie first appeared on stage at the age of fifteen in a City Road tavern. Her career began in 1885 and encompassed a period of great social turbulence for women. She rose to become an international star at a time when women were pelted with refuse for asserting their independence, and abused for their outspokenness. It seems strange that men from all sides of society, who denied their own wives and lovers simple freedoms, worshipped a woman who earned many times their annual salaries by her talent and tough handling of powerful variety managers.

The theatre has always been a world apart, as though years of creating fantasy have somehow imbued it with its own mystique and laws, like a kingdom within a kingdom. This sense of being totally dependent on the mainstream of life, yet removed from the common tide was perhaps never stronger than in the days of pre-World War I Variety. Outside the Empires, Alhambras and Coliseums the suffragette movement reached threatening proportions as women took to the streets to promote their cause, often breaking the law in the process. Inside, the ladies of the stage, cocooned in a smokey land of belly-laughs and tearful ballads, experienced few of their sisters' problems. According to the law of Variety, if not the law of the land, they had complete equality with the men who worked alongside them. In theatre terms one working turn deserved the same treatment as another; there was no sexual pecking order.

A sanctuary of sorts for both suffragettes and variety girls sprang up in the unlikely setting of a terraced house in Hanley, in the Potteries, when Mrs Marsden, a well-known local theatrical landlady decided to join the movement. Her homely digs offered accommodation to both working showgirls and middle-class suffragettes on public-speaking tours.

'Mother joined them after seeing an advertisement in the paper,' her son Frank recalls. 'She didn't do anything desperate herself, apart from attending meetings in the market square. But she would run bathfuls of hot water ready for when the suffragettes came home. I used to wonder why they wore such long mackintoshes in the hot summer weather, and then I realized why. When they came home they were covered with rotten eggs and tomatoes and goodness knows what. They wouldn't come straight indoors, but knock on the window first. Mother would say:

Suffragettes, January election 1910.

"Go and open the back gate, Frank." Then they would undress in the shed at the back and come straight in for a bath.' Late at night, when the variety girls came home to rub their aching feet and drink cocoa round the kitchen range they would sit into the small hours chatting with their well-heeled fellow-guests. Sadly, there is no record of what they talked about – it might have been absorbing reading.

An interesting first-hand view of social attitudes inside and outside Variety was experienced by Vera Blades, whose mother sang on the boards. 'The theatre was not considered very glamorous in those days,' she says, 'but it was considered different.

Men and women would come off-stage after their act and stand at the side completely as equals, in the same way that circus people look at themselves. There was a certain courtesy extended to the ladies, but I never got the impression that they were treated as anything but equal. It was a very competitive business, but people like Nellie Wallace or Harry Lauder got on irrespective of their sex, just on their own merit. The theatre world had a much more advanced way of life. Artists lived then as the public live now.

'I was brought up ahead of my time, and I would say that I was quite emancipated from being very young. I was brought up in a good, natural manner; we talked openly about all kinds of things, from sex to money and fashion and, in turn, I had a very balanced childhood. I never had problems attributed to teenagers. I was one of the lucky ones and, as time passed, I did the same with my son.

'My circle of friends say I've had an interesting life; maybe I have, but it was a hard one. My mother went to an ordinary school, but she was an intelligent woman. She could have been a teacher, but there were no opportunities then. Instead she went out into the world and, as a result, my life has been different to most of my contemporaries.'

Most variety artists acted the fool to some degree on stage, but behind the greasepaint they were a resilient breed. Women who toured the halls, making their own travel and accommodation arrangements, and moving from town to town by train unescorted, showed a singular independence. Convention was not quite ready for it and Edwardians, like their Victorian forefathers, felt uneasy at the prospect of assertive women with minds, and wills, of their own. Applauding their antics from the safety of the circle was one thing, admiring their courage another.

When the suffragettes (a term coined by the *Daily Mail* to differentiate from law-abiding suffragists) began a campaign of violence, it was more than the establishment could stand. The *Daily Express*, in a long leader, demanded that troublesome women should be shipped to St Helena. The blustering article reflected a great anxiety about women's independence; to *Express* readers, at least: 'These women demand the rights of men,' it whinnied. 'Let them, then, be treated as men are treated in similar circumstances. They take advantage of their sex infirmities, and they

Suffragettes demonstrate in Victoria Park, 25 May 1913.

escape the punishment they rightly merit. If, then, we were too soft-hearted to permit a suffragette criminal's suicide in prison, let us do the next thing. DEPORT THEM! Send them to St Helena and keep them there. What was good enough for Napoleon ought to be good enough for Mrs Pankhurst and her crazy followers. This is no idle suggestion. It's feasible and sound. St Helena is a long way off. There is plenty of room, and few ships call there. The women could be made to work, and as means of escape are almost nil, the wholesome example of deportation would soon put an end to the women for whom notoriety is as the breath of their nostrils.'

The *Express*'s wholesome suggestion was wisely ignored, and the spate of bombings and vandalism continued. Women ultimately won the vote as much by their nuisance value as by the justice of their cause, though their attacks were not as wantonly anarchistic as some reports suggested. Flora Drummond, one of the original handful of suffragettes, looked back on the tactics of the women's movement just before her death: 'We set fire to churches, homes, pillar boxes and so on, to force the insurance companies to influence the government to give us the vote. There was a good deal of method in our madness. We did not destroy any property unless we knew it was well insured. We were forced to do it. Destroying property affected the well-to-do classes, but we burnt pillar boxes to influence the man in the street.'

Flora, 'an exceedingly small, plump woman with apple cheeks and a turned-up nose, brimful with merriment and high spirits,' was dubbed General Drummond within the movement; riding in military uniform at the head of campaign marches, with an officer's cap and epaulettes. She was born on the Isle of Arran and qualified as a postmistress, but was disqualified from holding a job when she failed to pass the government's minimum height regulations. Despite a record of many arrests

Flora was always on cheerfully good terms with the police, and was actually having dinner at Scotland Yard during a suffragette raid on the House of Commons.

Her colleagues – 'you could have put the whole suffrage movement in a cab in the beginning,' she recalled – were of similar character. As a bunch they were tough, educated women who, by persuasion and example, recruited thousands of supporters from industrial towns and country villages, bringing out qualities that many were surprised to find they had. Despite a broadside of spluttering editorials their courage and humanity changed public opinion as the Great War approached. Old opponents, moved to admiration by their single-mindedness and dedication, repeated Asquith's comment about Edith Cavell: 'There are thousands of such women, but a year ago we did not know it.'

THE WORKING ladies of the stage may not have held such passionate political convictions – their need for them was less pressing – but they were of an equally singular character. Variety singers and comediennes may not have wrecked the orchid house at Kew, attacked opponents with horse whips, or tossed hatchets into the open carriages of visiting politicians, but their power and influence was marked with a similar steely determination.

Successful artists had strong personalities and a blazing independence, fuelled by seemingly endless creative energy. In 1912 women songwriters dominated sheet music sales, compared with the handful in today's music industry. Perhaps it was a driving desire to succeed when the odds were stacked so heavily against them. Women wrote for male performers with great success: Teresa de Riego's *Oh, Dry Those Tears* – an enormous hit of the period – sold 60,000 copies of sheet music in little

Pamela Stevenson plays
Lily Ferris.

more than the first month of publication.

As the climate was not entirely in their favour, some used male pen names, such as Guy d'Hardelot who wrote the immensely popular *I Know A Lovely Garden*; lyricist Laurence Hope, famous in her day for Indian Love Lyrics, was married to a general. Some were classical musicians who saw an expanding market in popular songs, and turned their talents to a quick killing – Frances Allitsen graduated from the Guildhall School of Music, and her compositions *There's A Land* and *A Song Of Thanksgiving* were hits on both sides of the Atlantic. Among her competitors were Florence Aylward, who had been a brilliant child pianist, and Dorothy Forster who abandoned an established career as a concert pianist to gamble on writing popular ballads.

Artists bought their songs, along with the exclusive right to sing them, often building long careers around the works of anonymous songwriters. At the turn of the century Lottie Collins bought *Ta-Ra-Ra-Boom-De-Ay*! for ten shillings with a view to possibly trying it in her act. It was still being sung around the world long after World War I.

The serio-comiques of Variety added a lustre to the era with ballads which were whistled and hummed on top of buses and at kitchen sinks around the country – Alice Lemar's *Her Golden Hair Was Hanging Down Her Back* . . . Ella Shield's *Burlington Bertie* . . . *In Her Hair She Wore A White Camelia* by Maggie Duggan . . . Kate Carney's *Three Pots A Shilling* . . . Nellie Farrell's *As True As The Stars That Are Shining* . . . and Lottie Lennox's popular *Put On The Green Bonnet That You Wore At Dublin Fair* . . . represent a handful of them.

On stage the artists dressed as pictures of Edwardian elegance; soft, feminine beauties twirling parasols; women who looked the very antithesis of everything the suffragettes represented – until they opened their mouths. Some of the women's songs were considered shockingly blue and unfit for decent company; a point which did not deter rich and poor alike from packing theatres wherever they performed. Even the sweetest songs were delivered with risqué intonation. Bonnie Kate Harvey, a music hall queen of the wink and sly aside, was typical of the genre – the emphasis she poured into songs like *You See I'm But A Simple Country Maid* left little to the imagination.

Bessie Bellwood, who died at the height of her career in 1896, was a former Bermondsey rabbit skinner who, even in the words of her agent, 'did not have a great deal of innate delicacy in her mental make-up.' Her favourite number, delivered in raucous Cockney, was *What Cheer, Ria*! It endeared her so much to audiences that several thousand people lined the streets for her funeral:

> What Cheer Ria! Ria's on the job.
> What Cheer Ria! Did you speculate a bob?
> Oh Ria, she's a toff and she looks immenskoff,
> And they all shouted, What Cheer, Ria!'

Bessie was one hundred per cent Music Hall, shouting back at hecklers and suggestively belting out songs, such as *The Organ*

*What Cheer 'Ria* sung by Bessie Bellwood.

*Grinding Girl* and *Has Anyone Seen My Mary Ann?* Jerome K. Jerome was among the audience for her opening performance at the Star, Bermondsey, where Bessie – on home ground – was in fine form. He reported for *The Idler*: 'She was at once heckled by a hefty-looking coal heaver who made it clear that he had no intention of allowing his drinking to be disturbed. A slanging match ensued with Bessie declaring her intention of "wiping the bloomin' hall with him and making it respectable." For over five minutes she let fly, leaving him gasping, dazed and speechless. At the end, she gathered herself together for one supreme effort, and hurled at him an insult so bitter with scorn, so sharp with insight into his career and character, so heavy with prophetic curse, that strong men drew and held their breath while it passed over them, and women hid their faces and shivered. Then she folded her arms and stood silent, and the house, from floor to ceiling, rose and cheered her until there was no more breath left in its lungs.'

Marie Lloyd, who took over her crown, approached her audience less like a bull at a barn door, but was as generous with her earnings as 'our own Bess' had been. As Marie's career progressed she commanded fees of up to £600 a week, but left nothing when she died – all the money had been given to the poor and needy. Marie, Bessie and Florrie St John, another music hall comedienne from a working class family, gave more than simply money. They would spend their spare time in East End tenement blocks, cleaning rooms for the elderly living alone or visiting the sick, sitting on their beds to chat and keep them company. Much of this private side of their lives was unknown to the general public. It was generous in the extreme; how much was tinged with guilt or conscience we shall never know. Bessie Bellwood would retire to church after a blazing backstage row and pay to have masses said for those she had quarrelled with.

Marie used to travel to Brinsworth, the home for retired variety artists, after a show and tip her fee on to the table to share among them, before singing a selection of their favourite songs and leaving in the early hours. When she died, an old music hall performer wrote to critic Chance Newton of the *Referee*: '. . .this is a blooming sad Saturday night for poor pro's, I give yer *my* word. No Marie, my boy, no little Marie with her little bag, giving out her usual bits of money to the hard-up-uns. My God! What a Saturday night for *them*, eh, sonny.'

Charlotte Glover, forty years a dresser at the Old Met music hall, referred to another, nameless singer who concealed her selflessness. 'She was a famous woman entertainer who had an invalid husband to whom she was very attached. During a long and anxious period she was compelled, in order to provide for his treatment, to appear on the boards every night. The couple were not well off. All their savings had gone on doctors' bills, and she could not afford to miss a single performance. Every night she appeared in her part, smiling, convulsing the audience with laughter, yet the moment the curtain was drawn for the last time she would fall into my arms and sob pitiably.'

Such noble sentiments were in keeping with an image of womanhood which had emerged among the mid-Victorian middle classes. Mrs Beeton, though quite revolutionary in championing women's independence, encouraged charitable works; and a belief that women should play a passive role continued through the Edwardian era. Marie, Bessie and co, were from a completely different stratum of society and unlikely to have been influenced by such chauvinism, but the image of womanhood nevertheless played an important role on the variety and music hall stage.

Bert Errol, acclaimed as the best female impersonator of his day, based his act on the costume style of society beauties, with an elegance which seemed devoid of camp. His singing voice, which could veer from trilling falsetto to gutsy tenor, added to his popularity, but audiences were mainly fascinated by his accurate studies of famous Edwardian ladies. Errol's act evolved from the temperamental black-faced prima donnas he portrayed in early minstrel shows. His performance attracted so much attention that he switched the make-up from black to white, abandoned burlesque songs for straight ballads and concentrated on building a wardrobe of expensive, feather-trimmed evening gowns. Like his successor, Danny La Rue, he also gave stunningly accurate impersonations of famous female singing stars for the amusement of his appreciative audience.

MUSIC HALL, for all its cheeky humour, was a conservative medium, reflecting the stance of everyday people. Male comics had a long tradition of sharing a joke with their audiences at any sign of women's independence. Herbert Campbell, a loud 127 kg (20 st) comedian who made his name appearing in panto opposite Dan Leno, ridiculed the 'new woman'. One song – *At My Time Of Life* – was so popular that it kept him in steady work at different halls each night for several years, a testament to the conservatism of his audiences. Dressed as a rather dowdy middle-aged Mrs Average, he sang:

> Fancy me a-smoking fags
> A-riding bikes and wearing 'bags',
> And leaving off my bits of 'rags'
> At my time of life.

Others, like Whit Cunliffe, the last of the 'lions comiques', or 'heavy swells', spent a career singing the praises of girls who behaved as girls were expected to:

> . . . What is it makes the girls so bright and breezy,
> Longing to be cuddled everywhere?
> What is it makes 'em teasable,
> Squeezable? It's feasible
> It's something in the seaside air.

However, the women they worked alongside in the variety theatres of Britain – in many cases bigger and more illustrious stars than they were ever to become – were far from demure and perfect. Despite their appearance as delicate, Sickert-like ladies in swirling dresses, they conducted their private lives with a single-mindedness which shattered fragile Edwardian values. The idea of women making their own way in a stage career, however, proved irresistably attractive to well-heeled young men who had led cloistered lives at public school and were killing time to inherit the family fortune. They clustered around stage doors like moths around the flame of bright sexuality exuded by carefree, dazzling girls who loved the attention.

Several actresses married into titled families, unions eased by the Prince of Wales' well-publicized affair with Lillie Langtry and Sarah Bernhardt's popularity in wealthy society. Outstanding beauties with tumbling hair and porcelain faces were soon exchanging vows – in discreet secrecy – with fresh-faced young aristocrats. John Fisher charted the chronology of some of the leading lights in his *World Of The Forsythes*:

'Rosie Boote from Tipperay – her hit song was *Maisie Gets Right There* – married the 4th Marquis of Headfort, whom she had met at a garden party in April 1901: the first such alliance to take place in the new century. The wedding was held in great secrecy at Saltwood, a village near Hythe, Kent. Next, there was Eva Chandler, who appeared under the stage name of Eva Carrington. She met the 25th Lord de Clifford in 1904 when she was playing on tour at the Gaiety Theatre, Dublin, in 'The

Catch Of The Season'. His lordship returned from Cairo in 1906 to marry his beloved by special licence at Holborn Town Hall.

'Then there was Miss Camille Clifford who, in 1904, had been christened the Gibson Girl because she came nearest the conception of the perfect woman as seen by the American artist, Charles Dana Gibson. The Gibson Girl was a statuesque goddess, her hair piled up in three enormous billows with, perhaps, an oyster shell hat on top, skewered on with pins. Her dress would be worn either completely off the shoulders, or linked to them only with token shoulderstraps. The waist was constricted to give an hour-glass effect exaggerating the size of the hips below, and of the bosom above, and although the latter was somewhat constrained by the new, so-called "straight front corset", the upper half of the Gibson Girl reminded some observers of a ship's figurehead. Camille secretly married the Hon. Henry Lyndhurst Bruce, the eldest son of the second Baron Aberdare in the same year. (There were ructions in the family when the secret leaked out.)

'Miss Jessie Smither, who had appeared under the stage name of Denise Orme at Daly's in "The Little Michus", married the Hon. John Reginald Yarde-Buller, the 2nd Baron Churston's heir in April 1907. She reappeared at the Gaiety in 1909 in "Our Miss Gibbs" (in which the heroine was a

Camille Clifford.

shop girl) but retired the following year when her husband came into the title. Sylvia Storey, who had acted since she was six years old, married the 7th Earl Pouett at St James', Piccadilly, in September 1908 while she was still in the cast of "Havanna" at the Gaiety, and Olive May, whose real name was Meatyard, married Lord Victor Paget, younger brother of the 6th Marquess of Anglesey, in January 1913.'

A formidable list, and one which served to enhance the appeal of actresses. Their allure was given a further boost by photography, which promoted the cult of the beautiful star; carefully posed photographs of actresses draped like alabaster goddesses flooded Edwardian magazines. It was the heyday, too, of the picture postcard and female variety entertainers made a profitable sideline from pocket publicity pictures which sold in their thousands in corner shops and department stores. Women, with looks beyond the dreams of ordinary folk, smiled hauntingly from enamel advertising hoardings, newspapers and sheet music covers.

The girls of Variety were a singular breed. Some of them, such as Vesta Tilley, had successful marriages to titled husbands, but there was a distinct social difference between the champagne-sipping Gaiety Girls and the painted ladies of the halls. Working people idolized their attractive heroines because they had the common touch; and the girls, in turn, had a healthy disregard for convention.

MARIE LLOYD displayed a natural open-handedness in all things, particularly her love affairs, which made her a constant target for gossip. In 1904, when her first husband, Percy Courtney, a race-horse punter, divorced her for adultery she was living with someone else and making

Carefully posed photographs of actresses draped like alabaster goddesses flooded Edwardian magazines.

no attempt to hide it. Marie even posed for newspaper photographs, in lace-trimmed dress and feather hat, reading the divorce court summons. The picture did little to improve the reputation of variety girls.

She eventually married her lover, Cockney comedian Alec Hurley. He was a former fairground boxer who sang down-to-earth songs such as *I Ain't Nobody In Particular*. Marriage seemed to take the excitement out of their affair, and they agreed to part a few years after the wedding in 1906. Hurley died in 1913, just before the divorce was finalized. Marie's life was like her songs – honest, almost innocent and delivered in a way which concealed little. Her reputation travelled ahead of her – when a Midlands watch committee insisted that she sang her entire repertoire before she was allowed to appear at their local theatre, Marie obliged. She performed stone-faced, without a wink or a grin and the committee, wondering if the rumours could really have been true, passed every number.

'Now,' said Marie, striding round the committee room when she had finished, 'you've heard my songs – I want to hear one of *your* songs. Take that little ballad *Come Into The Garden Maud*. Your wives often sing it – doesn't it go like this. . .' and she launched into it with a suggestively cocked eyebrow, a shrug of the shoulders and a knowing grin. 'Before she had

finished,' said one account 'every manjack of the committee was fiery red to the ears.'

'She was dear to the crowd,' St John Ervine said of her, 'because she was the essence of the crowd . . . She overflowed . . . She gave a word its value. One of Marie Lloyd's winks was as full of meaning as a dictionary. Her hesitations were eloquent. There was more laughter in her pauses than in other people's words.'

She was born Tilly Wood, and began her working life helping her father who made artificial flowers for an Italian in North London. Marie, the eldest of eleven children, had no stage training apart from dancing as a girl to a street corner barrel organ. Her first job outside the family business was in a boot factory, which

*Everything in the Garden's Lovely* song-sheet.

lasted exactly a week. She had a rebellious streak, tempered by a cheery nature, but employers found her expansive personality difficult to handle. Marie's second job, as a feather-curler in the fashion trade, also lasted a week. At the third factory, where she was taken on as an apprentice bead-trimmer, she was sacked for misbehaviour. When the forewoman was called to the office the girls dared Marie to dance on the workbench. She was still hoofing when the forewoman returned. The incident made up her mind to try for a job in music hall.

At fifteen she was appearing at the Grecian Assembly Rooms for fifteen shillings (75p) a week, billed as Bella Delmare. Within a year it had risen to £10, and an agent suggested that she should change her name. Tilly liked Marie, and then saw a billboard advertising *Lloyd's Weekly Newspaper* – The Family Oracle. 'I told him Marie Lloyd,' she said. 'That's me from now on.' One manager, with a penchant for alliteration, billed her as 'The Tasty, Trippy, Twiggy, Timely, Telling, Tender, Tempting, Toothsome, Transcendent, Trim, Tactical, Twinkling, Tricksy, Triumphal, Tantalizing, Tricky Little Trilby.'

By the following year she was commanding £100 a week and a benefit show was staged for her eighteenth birthday in the West End. Marie spent some of the money on clothes, including a black leather motoring suit – considered the height of fashion – which her brother was ordered to clean regularly with boot polish until it gleamed like ebony. With the rest of the benefit takings she bought eighty pairs of lace-up boots for children at her old school in the East End. Marie gave a large proportion of her earliest earnings to the under-privileged, and continued to do so with every fee she received – an estimated £250,000 in her lifetime. She always carried two draw-string bags in her handbag – one full of gold coins, the other silver – to give away. Destitute East Enders would crowd

the stage door with hard-luck stories. 'Don't tell me – I don't want to hear,' she would say, but before she reached the waiting cab her pouches would be empty.

The money rolled in because Marie had an obsessive drive to succeed, even if it meant treading on toes. One of her early, and most popular numbers, was *The Boy I Love Is Up On The Gallery*, which she blatantly stole from the widely-liked Nellie Power. When Nellie cornered her and delivered an unrestrained tongue-lashing, Marie tactfully phased out the song from her act and bought exclusive material to suit her own personality.

Her third husband was Derby-winning jockey Bernard Dillon, eighteen years her younger, with whom she had lived, openly as ever, for several years. In 1913, before they married, Marie left for a tour of America and Canada, where she became one of the very few British variety artists of the era to win acclaim. Dillon travelled with her and shared her cabin during the crossing. When they docked, the U.S. Department of Immigration made it clear that it took a dim view of unmarried couples, however famous, posing as man and wife, and incarcerated them on Ellis Island. As they kicked their heels in their respective cells, a deportation order accusing them of immorality was being signed by the chief immigration officer. Marie, with a prestigious tour at stake, made strenuous efforts to have the order revoked. On the eleventh hour it was rescinded to £600 bail on condition that they signed a promise not to co-habit in the United States.

Everything about Marie Lloyd made good newspaper copy, and Edwardian papers with a taste for sensation duly obliged. Marie dominated show business gossip pages, but was by no means the only eccentrically independent woman to offend social attitudes. Lesser artists gained a reputation for risqué performances, though their private lives were not as tempestuously eventful as the 'Queen of Comediennes'.

Zaeo, a muscular young lady from Norwood, trained as a circus trapeze artist, giving aerial displays in many countries. Back in London, where late-Victorian gentlemen found her performances rivetting, the sight of a woman in a lacey leotard and tights was a titillating novelty. Zaeo, however, did not appeal to everyone – when she was booked to appear at Westminster's Royal Aquarium as a special attraction, fly-posters were plastered all over London showing her in her working costume. The formidable Central Vigilante Society for the Repression of Immorality accused her of public indecency, and a worried theatre manager hastily had the advertising removed.

Zazal, a contemporary who also appeared at the Aquarium, was a coiffeured human cannonball who favoured satin cami-knickers and a low-slung bodice. There was outraged indignation wherever she performed with her twenty-four inch howitzer; but the objections served only to increase the crowds which gathered to watch her sail heroically into her safety net. Even the great outdoors could no longer be considered safe from scantily-clad ladies. Ada Webb, 'The Queen Of The Crystal Tank', dressed in what, at the turn of the century, was the most revealing swimsuit. Ada plunged from the piers of British holiday resorts, even in the coldest weather, and performed graceful antics on stage in a glass-sided water tank.

WOMEN VARIETY artists – saucy though they were – appealed equally to women because of the heavy love interest in their songs. Vesta Victoria, for instance, described by music hall historian Roy Busby as 'the prototype of the dumb blonde', built a career on numbers which would have provided ample material for Mills and Boon. Her theme was unrequited love – in every possible permutation – from *Daddy Wouldn't Buy Me A Bow-Wow*, delivered in a little-girl voice, to her other enduring hit *Waiting At The Church*. Between these rather depressing milestones, Vesta sang countless songs of love affairs which always managed to turn into minefields of frustration and anxiety. *Poor John* was hugely popular at the height of the Edwardian era:

> John took me round to see his mother!
> His mother! His mother!
> And while he introduced us to each other,
> She weighed up everything that I had on.
> She put me through a cross-examination;
> I fairly boiled with aggravation.
> Then she shook her head, looked at me and
>     said:
> Poor John! Poor John!

In marriage, too, she was destined to lose; and audiences, anticipating the inevitable punch lines, would roar them out in unison. None more loudly than *Waiting At The Church*, which ended:

> . . . When I found he'd left me in the lurch,
> Lor! How it did upset me!
> All at once, he sent round a note,
> Here's the very note, this is what he wrote:
> 'Can't get away to marry you today –
> My wife won't let me!'

While Vesta made a lucrative living as the wilting violet unlucky in love, other female variety stars pulled no punches when it came to opinions on men. Their songs were aimed at working class women whose husbands rolled home drunk, or spent the last of the housekeeping on ale. Sung from woman to woman it struck a common chord and contributed enormously to the singer's popularity. Jenny Hill, 'The Vital Spark', delivered her songs hands on hip, washerwoman style, and sang with the voice of experience. Her husband, a music hall acrobat who found married life hard to adjust to, walked out on her soon after the birth of their daughter. One of her songs went:

> He's out on the fuddle, with a lot of his
>     pals,
> Out on the fuddle along with other gals;
> He's always on the fuddle, while I'm in
>     such a muddle.
> But I mean to have a legal sep-ar-ation!

Jenny, who did not live to see the turn of the century, has been acclaimed one of the great talents of music hall. Like Marie Lloyd she identified instinctively with her audiences with a flair for extravagance which they loved. She loved to ride through Paddington, where she was born, in her carriage with its twin lamps, each bearing the slogan The Vital Spark.

Ada Reeve, who made a successful transition from pre-war variety to musical comedy and films, came from a poor background but, unlike her contemporaries, managed to avoid the excesses of the free and easy theatre life. Before her death at the age of ninety-two, she looked back on the heyday of the halls and admitted: 'Of course there *were* young men at the stage doors and there were after theatre suppers. I wasn't particularly pretty, but my engagement book was always full three weeks ahead. Nothing indecorous, though. The boys seemed to like to take me out – I once had two future Lords of the Admiralty in tow – but they behaved beautifully. I was always home by twelve.'

Ada's father was a 'utility gent', a jobbing actor from Mile End, who arranged her first audition at the age of six. She was lifted on to the kitchen table in pinafore and dress and told to recite a passage from *Henry VII* for a variety agent. She made her music hall debut with topical recitations, punctuated by cartwheels, to which the audience would call 'Over Ada!'. Like Marie Lloyd she was the eldest of a

large family, sixteen children in all. Her mother had been forced to abandon a dancing career to look after them and, although Ada had to help, her father seemed determined to launch her into music hall. Before she left home for the

Ada Reeve with her daughters.

theatre he would furiously scribble her recitations – on anything from Jack the Ripper to the price of fish – for the evening's performance.

Ada first earned £3 a week, which was not quite enough to buy *Daddy Wouldn't Buy Me A Bow-Wow*, offered to her for 5 guineas by songwriter Joe Tabrar. Vesta

Victoria, the not-so-dumb-blonde, quickly seized the opportunity and never looked back. Ada vowed never to be in a similar situation again, and borrowed £5 from an old flame she had jilted to buy *What Do I Care*. It became one of the great hits of the turn of the century, boosting her salary to £50 a week. She was singing it, and still performing her cartwheels, when George Edwardes of the Gaiety spotted her and signed her for one of his shows. Variety still beckoned, but Ada was strongly drawn to the West End, with its stage door Johnnies and heady atmosphere of champagne-in-slippers. She earned a good salary in the best theatres, but never quite stopped the show (that privilege was left to the manager of the Lyric, where she was appearing in *Florodora*, when he ran on-stage in 1900 during the second act and shouted: 'Ladies and gentlemen – Mafeking has been relieved!')

Ada lived through the great days of Variety when it mirrored the everyday life of the poor in comedy and song. Her talent prevented her from slipping back into the impoverished conditions of Mile End, but she was equally cautious not to allow her head to be turned by wealthy young Knuts. Ada had an earthy commonsense, yet was a romantic who always spoke kindly of the men in her life. Such sentiment found little sympathy in Variety, where the battle of the sexes – preferably with no holds barred – was always popular material. Women's songs about men were wry and accurate but the men sang about women in quite different terms.

A WIFE'S FUNCTION was portrayed as solely to take the fun out of life by complaining about nights out with the boys, counting the change and discovering marital indiscretions. Women were the butt of countless variety songs and jokes, and it is little surprise that Variety's vital sparks hit back with a vengeance. Music Hall was not considered entertainment suitable for ladies by the Victorians – but by the Edwardian era Variety was widely patronized by women who cheered the girls on stage when they sang disparagingly about men.

Charles Godfrey, a top-hatted 'swell' swinging a silver-tipped cane, made his money singing patriotic songs, but occasionally switched targets from the Hun to the other common enemy, women. After spending his money on drink in *The Blessings of Marriage*, he sang:

> My wife will start nagging, for no reason why.
> Blow me, if she does I won't stand it – not I.
> If she lets me have too much, she'll get a black eye,
> She will, and I don't care who knows it. . .

Marriage was a trap from which every man had a duty to escape – *She Was One Of The Early Birds, And I Was One Of The Worms*, *Poor Married Man*, and *Why Did I Leave My Little Back Room In Bloomsbury* were all popular ballads warning of the drawbacks of married life. Even Dan Leno, not noted for his misogyny jumped on the bandwagon with:

> Once I used to be so sad,
> Now I'm happy. Now I'm glad;
> With joy I think I shall go mad –
> For Mary Anne's refused me!

Tom Costello, who dressed in a straw boater, bow tie and stiff collar was requested to sing *At Trinity Church I Met My Doom* every night for almost a decade, until it became of the of the great variety classics:

> At Trinity Church I met my doom.
> Now I live in the top back room,
> Up to my eyes in debt for rent-y,
> That's what she's done for me!

It was unlikely that Costello, who lived very comfortably, was speaking from personal experience, but his wife was known to have her dominant moments. George Foster, his agent for twenty-five years, recalled: 'At one time he had "a few words with the missus", and she went to the length of locking him in the house until it was time to leave for his evening's round of the Tivoli, the Canterbury and the Oxford. Looking through the window, Tom saw a newsboy at the street corner wearing a bill on which were only two words in very big letters – FOSTER ILL.

'The reference was to the brilliant Worcester cricketer then playing for England against the Australians in the Test Match. "Great Scott, Nellie!" Tom shouted through the door. "Something awful's happened to poor George Foster. It's on the news bill. Look out and you'll see for yourself. I must go up to town and find out about old George!" Mrs Costello fell for the wheeze and Tom was released an hour or two before his sentence was up.'

Women answered with songs more witty and barbed, and aimed at applause from long-suffering wives. Some of the better examples sang in glowing praise of unimpeachable husbands, but there was always a sting in the tail. Vesta Victoria's widow's ballad, *He Was A Good Kind Husband*, always went down well when there were women in the audience:

> There he would sit by the fireside,
> Such a chilly man was John.
> I hope and trust there's a nice warm fire
> Where my old man's gone . . .

At the other extreme, a handful of songs, such as *My Old Dutch* or *I Want A Girl Just Like The Girl That Married Dear Old Dad*, oozed with sentiment and extolled the virtues of womanhood. The sex war continued in the streets as well as on the stage; but just as the suffragettes had allies in the House of Commons, women had their champions in Variety. The appropriately-named James Fawn wooed his audience with lines like: ' . . . here's to the fair sex, our sweethearts and wives; in spite of her faults she's the joy of our lives.' But he could not afford to break with tradition for too long. *Woman, Lovely Woman* ended:

> Who sticks to us like glue since the world
>   began?
> Who loves to cut a dash, who loves to
>   spend the cash?
> But who has to pay the damage? Man,
>   poor man!

WHILE MEN sang songs deriding women, some female artists astutely turned the tables by making careers as male impersonators. It was a subject considered more daring and laden with innuendo than female impersonation. There was already a long tradition of pantomime dames, and characters such as Bert Errol, with his society drag act, were both popular and acceptable. The idea of a woman dressing as a man in an age when the virtues of womanhood had to be displayed, always created discomfort in some circles. The Queen and her lady guests at the 1912 Command Performance, as we have seen, averted their eyes at the sight of Vesta Tilley impersonating a Piccadilly Johnnie. There were many women drag artists but, like their male counterparts, only those who could perform with a certain panache and sophistication became enduring successes. Even in an era of almost constant change and innovation, high camp was not an Edwardian fashion.

The 1890s are regarded by many as the golden age of the halls, and indeed most of the big stars had established their reputations by the turn of the century. But the fourteen years that followed, leading to the outbreak of war, brought the full blossoming of their talent in the livelier setting of Variety. The ragtime zest of the Edwardians reflected the new ground being broken all around in science and manufacturing – a climate of restless creativity which culminated in the best popular songs and performances in popular theatre. The surge of talent was ultimately subdued by the sound of gunfire but, like all great shows, it went out on a high note.

Vesta Tilley, the finest of the male impersonators, reached the peak of her popularity during this period, and was considered the ideal public figure to recruit young men into the forces. Drag achieved an eminence and official approbation which has eluded it ever since.

She continued to sing for the troops during the war years and later recalled how much life had changed: 'It had lost a lot of the zest and sparkle of the really good old days, but it was still lots of fun. Everyone was anxious to forget the war and have as good a time as possible. Prices had gone up in comparison with 1914, and we knew that we had seen the end of an era, but life still seemed good and full of promise.'

Vesta's father was a china painter at a Worcester pottery. In his spare time he played the piccolo while his puppy, Fathead, performed tricks. Eventually he made the break from factory life to manage a small music hall in Gloucester, taking his family with him. Vesta, or Matilda Powles as she was then, loved to sit alongside her father as he announced the turns as a chairman of the hall. They were soon touring together as Harry Ball the Tramp Musician and the Great Little Tilley. After a year or two Vesta began to worry that she was just like hundreds of other show-girls on the circuit.

'I felt that I could express myself better if I were dressed as a boy,' she said. 'One night after supper I kissed my father goodnight, and on my way to bed took his hat and overcoat from the rack in the lobby of the house and carried them to my bedroom. Instead of jumping into bed, tired as I was, I put on the coat, which trailed on the floor behind me, the hat, which I stuffed to prevent it falling over my eyes, and before the looking glass tried to sing the song I had heard, as the men sang it, with the appropriate manly action. So engrossed was I that I did not hear the door open, and sang on until I heard my father's voice. I was in an awful funk!

'I knew that he would be vexed with me for not being asleep in bed, but, bless him, he smiled and said: "That was quite good. Would you like to have a suit of boy's clothes for one of your songs?" Needless to say I was delighted and sure enough, later, I was the possessor of a little evening dress suit.'

Vesta had grown too big to be called the Great Little Tilley, and her father suggested that she should change her name. He scribbled three words on separate pieces of paper, put them into a hat and invited her to pick one out. She drew Vesta, and took an immediate liking to it. The suit, however, drew a different response. Her first appearance in it was at Leicester where she strode manfully on stage impersonating Sims Reeves, a popular tenor. The chairman, an eccentric old buffer named Paul, leapt to his feet and ordered the band to stop in the middle of the opening number. 'What are you doing in those trousers?' he bellowed at the diminutive Vesta. 'I engaged you as a little girl, not a boy. Take them off at once and put your skirt on!' Then, turning sweetly to the audience, he announced: 'Ladies and gentlemen, I regret this interruption, but the band will play a selection of popular tunes while Little Tilley returns to take off her trousers and appear as we expect to see her.' Tilley, who had turned a deep crimson, was led sobbing from the stage. On the last night of the week's run she was allowed to do just one turn in trousers. Her famous career had begun.

Vesta, like others born into variety

families, spent a childhood of late nights waiting for her parents to return from the theatre, or touring from town to town. Some might suggest that her urge to succeed compensated for a bleak childhood existence, but actor-manager J. Pitt Hardacre, who knew Vesta for many years saw it differently: 'Her childhood would seem to many to have been devoid of much pleasure or happiness,' he wrote in 1926, 'but it was not so. In every child possessing a spark of genius is the happiness gained from imagination, often unperceived by others, even its parents. Week after week in different rooms, no playmates, no regular school hours, the small child had to employ her time in her own fashion. Vesta Tilley's early days can be summed up in one word – dolls. Dolls, dolls and yet more dolls.

'Playing at keeping house under the parlour table with the table cloth hanging down round it, completing the illusion if its being the interior of a room, the child-actress spent almost all the time that she was away from the theatre. Probably it was the finest education that a child of her type could have had. In these quiet surroundings, who knows how her little brain was developing, and unconsciously laying the foundation of character studies with which she had delighted us?'

It was perhaps a fanciful notion, but not without a grain of truth. Vesta went on to create characters in her breezy act which are still fondly remembered. Their success was largely due to that strong imagination, and meticulous research which was quite unique in the bawdy, quick-fire world of Variety. During the war, for instance, she spent hours sitting on a bench at Victoria Station watching the troop trains come and go, before her first public performance of *Six Days Leave*, a song about homecoming Tommies. She studied the way they shouldered their rifles and kit bags and greeted their families before piecing together a perfect cameo.

Whether a Piccadilly toff, a policeman or

Recruiting drive on the variety stage.

Actress at recruitment show.

a fighting serviceman, her costumes were always tailored to the last detail. She overlooked nothing, even to selecting the cigars she smoked on stage. But behind the military precision, the textbook salutes and the swagger canes Vesta was essentially very feminine – a point instantly obvious to audiences who loved her because of it. When she sang at the recruitment rallies there was hardly a young man's heart who could refuse her appeal . . . plus the disturbing presence of children handing out white feathers to those who remained in their seats. *The Army Of Today's All Right*, she told them, and who would disbelieve 'England's finest recruiting sergeant'?

It's all right, it's all right now
There's no need to worry any more
Who said the army wasn't strong,
Kitchener proved them wrong
On the day he came along.

So let the band play, and shout 'Hooray!'
I'll show the Germans how to fight,
I joined the army yesterday
So the army of today's all right.

In 1920 she retired after half a century on the stage and settled down; but old habits died hard: 'Even now, about eight o'clock at night, I feel a certain excitement,' she wrote in her memoirs. 'This was the time for me to prepare for my performance in the old days and, less now I admit than formerly, I like to sneak off quietly to some secluded nook and dream again of the life I loved – the enthusiasm of the audience, the constant effort to give them almost more than I was physically capable of doing, the feeling of triumph and contentment after the performance, and the knowledge that it would all happen again the next night. Indeed, after my retirement, my health broke down, and I am certain it was because I could not rest content when the witching hour of the evening arrived.'

Vesta's contemporaries, Hetty King and Ella Shields, talented though they were, never quite achieved her perfection and flair. They obviously watched each other's acts closely. When Vesta sang *Burlington Bertie, The Boy With The Hyde Park Drawl*, Ella's husband William Hargreaves wrote *Burlington Bertie From Bow*, which became a great hit and one of the best-observed of the broken-down toff songs, Ella, from Baltimore, sang in a distinct American accent, which could not compete with Vesta's languid drawl, but in top hat and tails at least she looked the part.

Hetty King.

I'm Burlington Bertie
I rise at ten thirty and saunter along like a
   toff,
I walk down the Strand with my gloves on
   my hand
Then I walk down again with them off.
I'm all airs and graces, correct easy paces,
Without food so long I've forgot where my
   face is.
I'm Bert, Bert, I haven't a shirt,
But my people are well-off, you know!
Nearly ev'ry one knows me, from Smith to
   Lord Roseb'ry,
I'm Burlington Bertie from Bow.

Hetty King began her career as a child doing impersonations of Vesta Tilley. She appeared as Hetty Volta, with her father playing accordion, until her agent decided the name sounded like a Russian acrobatic troupe. By the age of thirteen she was appearing in Cinderella in Cardiff, setting an Edwardian record as the youngest bill-topper. Hetty divided her act between military and swell impersonations, and in World War I was still singing *All The Nice Girls Love A Sailor* for her troops. Hetty's popularity was boosted by mass circulation magazines, such as *Tit-Bits*, which devoted columns of gusty prose to her:

'Watch her fill a pipe sailor-fashion, cutting the twist, folding the jack-knife with one hand, lighting up leeward, flicking the match away breezily; then you'll understand why this finished artist is by no means finished as a public favourite.

Her soldier impersonations are equally polished, her drill movements faultless.

'Here's an authentic story told me by a Guard's officer: In a garrison town a drill sergeant had been working for half an hour on a very awkward squad of recruits. At last he gave it up in disgust. "Squad-shun!" he shouted. "Now today's pay day. When you've drawn your money, go to the Empire and see Hetty King. Perhaps she'll teach you how to handle a ruddy rifle – I can't!"'

A likely story – but, like today, readers would prefer to read anything about their favourite entertainers than nothing at all.

After fighting hard to establish their rights and independence, women were to prove their point dramatically by virtually running the country during the war. They took over the factories and farms, abandoning kitchen sinks and coming-out balls to roll up their sleeves and tackle jobs previously considered male preserves. Those too old or with other commitments knitted blankets and packed food parcels for the troops. The issue of votes for women was effectively shelved by the war, but they were enfranchised with alacrity when peace finally came. The girls who worked on stage during the long grey years between 1914 and 1918, and those who relaxed in the audiences enjoying the show had each fought for their independence in different ways, but the struggle had demanded equal courage and determination.

# ALMOST A
# GENTLEMAN

'Harry G. Burrard, The Eccentric Comedian who will have you Rolling in the Aisles.'

x

y

# ALMOST A
# GENTLEMAN

'Harry G. Burrard, The Eccentric Comedian who will have you Rolling in the Aisles.'

Joe Miller had the elastic face and hunted look which became the trade mark of a million comedians; from the moment he walked on stage the audience never quite knew what to expect. In the early 1700s, when he performed as a 'droll actor', there was no such thing as a stand-up comic. He was a working character actor, but a look, a gesture, an eccentric accent or an unscripted joke inevitably crept into whatever role he happened to be playing.

When he was buried at St Clement Danes in the Strand, in 1738, a bookmaker hurriedly issued a shilling pamphlet called *Joe Miller's Jests – The Wit's Vade Mecum*. It proved to be a gold mine, running to eleven editions in as many years, even though only three of the 247 'jests' could be reliably attributed to the tubby actor with the curly white wig and double chin. As comedy material it hardly sparkled, but audiences, through his performances, had developed a taste for visual and verbal quick-fire jokes. 'A midshipman, one night in company with Joe Miller and myself told us that being once in great danger at sea, everybody was observed to be on their knees,' wrote the bookie under the pseudonym Elijah Jenkins. 'But one man, who being called upon to come with the rest of the hands to prayers: "Not I," said he; "it is your business to take care of the ship; I am but a passenger."'

A century later, in the hands of the early music hall comedians who followed in his footsteps, it would have gone down like a lead balloon; but Miller made Georgian London roar with laughter. His epitaph, written by Stephen Duck, one of Queen Anne's favourite poets, read: 'Here lie the remains of honest Joe Miller, who was a tender husband, a sincere friend, a facetious companion and an excellent comedian . . .'

The great tradition of English humour has no direct line back to Miller, but he created a wry, satirical style of humour which is still popular today. Music Hall and Variety produced a collection of comedians who broadened comedy into distinctive styles, each with a quirky, whimsically British flavour which quickly disappeared after World War I. They were craftsmen of comedy, elevating timing to an art form, and flattening their audiences with sheer force of personality. The technique evolved from necessity; by 1914, variety spots were strictly timed and the comedian, marching on to face a full house without a microphone, had only minutes in which to hook and reel them in, like an angler playing an unpredictable pike. The great names, such as Billy Bennett, George Robey, Dan Leno and George Formby Senior, were at home before their audiences, performing with a graceful ease which made them idolized.

The art of making fickle audiences laugh was not easily acquired, but as most comics came from the same background, they knew instinctively how to play for applause. Their material ranged from the naïve rustic to the wildly surreal. 'In those days the working class wanted someone to look down on,' says Ernest Foy, nephew of Edwardian variety comedian Tommy Foy. 'I think it was because they were pretty down themselves. If they could see someone who was a little lower, or a bit dafter, it gave them a laugh.'

Foy, whose catch-phrase was 'Eee, I am a fool,' used a donkey in his act, presumably in the theory that it doubled his chances of a laugh. In company with many of his fellow artists, he was a time-served tradesman (the security of the day job was a great attraction), working as a sign writer in Halifax. At night he trained to be a circus acrobat, and later put his talents to work in a wide range of acts, from lightning cartoons to rodeo riding in a Wild West Show. It was only when he turned to comedy that he made any impression, and then only as a fool.

Foy won his first booking by pretending to be an Irishman – then, as now, unfortunately, a butt of English jokes. He played the part with such aplomb that he made the seemingly suicidal decision to tour Eire. He was a huge success, earning the ultimate accolade from a local newspaper: 'Foy is no stage Irishman, but a thorough Irishman with a brogue you could cut with a knife.' Back home, he reverted to Northern dialect jokes, and soon built such a following with his donkey, Balum, that he was urged to go to London. Foy was a shy man and the prospect terrified him, but Eugene Stratton, the black-face singer, finally persuaded him to take the plunge. Foy came to terms with his insecurity, and even capitalized on it, by thickening his accent and performing such numbers as *A Yorkshire Lad In London*. His trick was to appear more stupid than the donkey, and variety-goers loved it. As Priestley observed, the poorer the audience, the more desperate the laughter.

By the same token, the crazier the comedian, the wilder the reception. Billy Bennett, who looked like a cross between Adolph Hitler and an overstuffed Edwardian waiter, developed a dadaesque style which touched an anarchic streak in his working class audiences. Ken Dodd keeps his rather eccentric tradition alive with a scatter-gun humour based on bizarre juxtapositions (he originally billed himself as Professor Yaffle Chuckabutty, Operatic Tenor And Sausage Knotter).

BENNETT, also from Liverpool – it must be something in the Mersey air – revelled in the absurd with manic parodies of famous songs and poems. It was not entirely new, but no one had been shrewd enough, or daft enough, to take the style to such extremes before. *The Green Eye of the Little Yellow God*, for instance, was never quite the same again after the Bennett version, *The Green Tie of the Little Yellow Dog*:

> There's a cock-eyed yellow poodle to the
>    north of Waterloo,
> There's a little hot-cross bun that's turning
>    green.
> There's a double-jointed woman doing
>    tricks in Chu Chin Chow,
> And you're a better man than I am Gunga
>    Din . . .

Bennett bellowed his monologues agressively over the footlights, haranguing his audience with tortured versions of Kipling. His *Road to Mandalay* ran for years, with audiences never seeming to tire of the thirsty character in dusty tropical kit:

> There were no maps for soldiers
> In this land of Gunga Din,
> So they picked the toughest warrior out
> And tattoed on his skin.
> On his back he's got Calcutta,
> Lower down he's got Bombay,
> And you'll find him sitting peacefully
> On the road to Mandalay . . .

Critics have lyrically likened him to Lewis Carroll, Ionesco and Beckett. Bennett's own description of himself, beneath his name on the bills, is perhaps more appropriate – Almost A Gentleman. He was a burly ex-Lancer with a fierce Old Bill moustache; drooping trousers concertinad over hobnail boots; his stomach exploded through an ill-fitting tail-coat; a stiff shirt-front curled rebelliously like a roller-blind, while his neck, bulging over a waxed wing collar looked poised to burst a blood vessel. He always strolled on to his signature tune -- *She Was Poor But She Was Honest* -- a song which oozed Victorian sentiment and left the audience unprepared for the mayhem to follow:

> It's the same the whole world over,
> It's the poor what gets the blame,
> It's the rich what gets the pleasure --
> Isn't it a blooming shame.

His costume came about by accident, so the story goes. He left the army after serving as a professional soldier, and wore his uniform on stage singing military and patriotic songs. The highlight of his first week back in Civvy Street was an engagement at t he Theatre Royal, Dublin, where the manager took one look at him and, fearing a riot, advised him to change his clothes. Anti-British feeling was running high at the time, and the sight of a Tommy marching up and down the stage sing *It's A Long Way To Tipperary* was not the recipe for a quiet evening out. When Bennett confessed to the manager that he had no other clothes he was told to disguise his appearance so that he could, if necessary, be smuggled out of the building. The comedian desperately plastered down his hair into a quiff and stuck on a false moustache, which defused the situation by turning the solider into a figure of fun. When he returned to Liverpool the make-up stayed, but the uniform which had caused so much trouble was quickly replaced by an evening suit.

'I went into a second-hand shop in Liverpool and asked for an evening dress suit,' he said. 'The tailor produced one that had been made for a man my weight but many inches shorter. Consequently, when I tried it on there was a wide open space between the vest and the pants. "Just my fit," I said. The tailor thought I was crazy. To humour me, he said: "Now sir, a red silk handkerchief will complete the impression of a perfect gentleman." "Good, I'll buy one -- the largest you have, please," I said. He goggled slightly as I ordered my day suit to be sent to my address. Then I walked out of the shop in my curious outfit straight to the theatre to put on my new act.'

Subtlety was not a word in Bennett's vocabulary, but off-stage he loved to tell wry tales of his experiences. When he was booked to tour South Africa he found in Pretoria that the management had cashed in on his reputation by raising ticket prices. After the opening performance a disgruntled civic dignitary called at Bennett's hotel and complained that he normally got into the Grand for two shillings (10p), and had suddenly found himself being asked for two and sixpence (12½p). 'And frankly,' he added, 'I don't think you're worth the extra tanner.' Bennett was amused and replied, 'Well we'll soon settle that!' and airily slapped sixpence on the bar. The comedian walked through for dinner, quietly chuckling to himself while the dignitary collected his money and stalked out. 'But imagine my surprise,' Bennett said, 'when I went to leave the hotel an hour or so later, to find a queue two hundred strong all waiting for tanners.'

He wrote his first monologue at the age of nine when each member of the class was asked to sing or recite something specially for Christmas. Bennett used to recall how his teacher sat in frozen astonishment as he climbed on to the desk and chanted:

> Haul in the anchor
> Throw out the sail.
> Never tie a knot
> In a bulldog's tail.
> As long as I remember
> I never shall forget
> To use an um-ber-ella
> When it comes on wet.

This burgeoning talent led to surreal Bennett classics such as *It Was Christmas*

*Day In The Cookhouse*, and *A Sailor's Farewell To His Horse*, which Edward Lear would have loved – one of the whimsical couplets went: 'The little sardines had gone into their tins/ And pulled down the lids for the night.'

Bennett, unlike many other comedians, was a man of simple pleasures who spent his spare time playing golf or driving his car. Some, by contrast, cultivated quite serious off-stage interests. Will Hay was a Fellow of the Royal Astronomical Society and discovered spots on Saturn in 1933; George Robey was an acknowledged expert on philately; Wee Georgie Wood became a classicist who lectured on the life of Socrates (a fact he once mentioned to a fellow comic, who replied: 'I haven't played there for years.' 'Played where?' Georgie asked, rather puzzled. 'Stockton-on-Tees,' said the comedian).

THERE WAS yet another aspect of Variety characterized by the comedians who could afford no time for relaxation; down-bill clowns who hammered away at every booking their agents could acquire in a restless quest for fame. They became familiar, popular faces on the circuits, but lacked the elusive spark of genius which fell to but a few. It was an empty life of hard work, exhausting travel, bleak hotels, and occasionally an unpropitious end. Perhaps, least fortunate were those whose star had faded in the slipstream of fast-moving fashion when Variety passed its peak; their names are forgotten, their lives unrecorded. The sad story of Charles Dillon was one of the few which caught a sympathetic journalist's eye. Dillon was a comedian who 'knocked 'em dead' with an ever-ready quip and comic song before the Great War, only to die in obscurity. In 1918 he was one of the first artists to volunteer for the army; four years later, when he was discharged, it was as though he had stepped into another age. Dillon received assistance from the Variety Artists' Benevolent Fund, but slid deeper into poverty.

In 1934, the *Daily Mail* devoted a whole column to his death: 'Charles Dillon died at the age of 68 in a Highgate hospital after refusing to have a doctor, so as to avoid putting an extra burden of expense on his wife, who shared his fight with poverty.

'For the past nine years he and his wife have lived in a small furnished room in Islington for which they paid only a few shillings a week. But they had a sad time of it trying to find those few shillings to keep a roof over their heads.

"Thirty years ago we had all the money we could possibly wish for," said Mrs Dillon sadly; "those were the times when Charles was one of the most famous pantomime dames in London.

"But these years since the war have brought us harder and harder times. Lately, my husband did what little crowd work he could get in films, and occasionally he would get a small engagement in his old work.

"The old Tivoli, the Pavilion, the Oxford – all those fine old music halls knew my husband and me. We worked on the same bills as Marie Lloyd and all the other great stars of that time, and they were our friends, and for the thirty-nine years of our married life Charles and I were never parted.

"We used to work together in the halls, doing single turns. I was a serio-comic, and he did his patter and all the popular comic songs. He used to get a laugh the moment he came on – he always gave a plaintive sort of baa, like a sheep. Charles and I tried to adapt ourselves to the times, but the old names mean nothing to modern managers."

A spokesman for the Variety Artists' Benevolent Fund said: "To the last Mr Dillon was a brave, fine character. His clothes were worn, but they always looked

'The Funniest Man in England, The
Uproarious and Popular Tommy Beamish.'

neat and clean. Mr Dillon still looked a fine
man. He was tall, dark and much more
handsome than the average comedian.'"

Charles Dillon, 'the man who made
thousands laugh', possibly saw more
agents' waiting rooms and audition halls
than anyone of his generation. The tragic
private lives of famous comedians are a
well-worn cliché, but seldom more poignantly true than in the years straddling the
Great War. Was there ever a time when the
future seemed less certain, audiences so
fickle, and the whole character of an era
changed with such bewildering rapidity.
All artists want to be loved, and when a
brittle public turns its attention elsewhere,
the experience can be devastating.

THE MADCAP comedian, T. E.
Dunville, immensely popular
before the war, enjoyed a variety
career spanning thirty years. He
toured the provinces delivering jaunty
comic songs in evening dress, and found
that switching to a clown's red nose, loud
check suits and big boots appealed more to
his audience. Dunville boosted his earnings
by specializing in nonsense songs with
enigmatic titles such as *Dinky Dee, Bunk-
Adoodle-I-Do* and *Pop Pop Popperty Pop*,
which had unsophisticated audiences rolling in the aisles.

Then, as with many of his profession,
the chasm created by the war made it
impossible to pick up the threads of his old
act again. By 1918 the same crowds were
queuing for musical revues, and Dunville
found it difficult to adjust to the slick,
smart new comedy styles. He struggled to
find work and, after a down-bill appearance at the Grand Theatre, Clapham, was
referred to by one newspaper as 'a fallen
star.' A few days later, deeply depressed,
he waded into the Thames at Reading and
drowned hmself.

Mark Sheridan, who ended his life in a
Glasgow park, was a household name in
Edwardian days, and one of the most
popular comic singers of the period. He
was a talented performer who sang enduring songs, such as *Who Were You With Last
Night*, in a gusty fashion, pacing the stage
like a caged beast and giving the backdrop
hearty whacks with his umbrella as he
belted out the lyrics. The audience loved to
join in the choruses as he pranced about
with boundless energy in the autumn of
1914, singing *Here We Are, Here We Are,
Here We Are Again!* – his hat cocked at a
jaunty angle and bell-bottomed trousers
flapping wildly. Weeks later it was adopted
by departing troops as one of their
favourite marching songs.

He crystallized the optimism of the age,
summing up the Edwardians' love of
simple pleasures with his classic *I Do Like*

*To Be Beside The Seaside*, first performed in 1909. Public bathing, and the health-giving properties of sea water had become a national passion, which Sheridan joined a long line of singers in celebrating:

> Everyone delights to spend their summer holiday
> Down by the side of the silvery sea.
> I'm no exception to the rule – in fact, if I'd my way,
> I'd reside by the side of the silvery sea.
>
> But when you're just the common-or-garden Smith, Jones or Brown
> At bus'ness up in town, you've got to settle down;
> You save up all the money you can till summer comes around,
> Then away you go to a spot you know
> Where the cockle shells are found . . .
>
> Oh, I do like to be beside the seaside,
> I do like to be beside the sea.
> I do like to stroll upon the prom, prom, prom,
> Where the brass bands play "Tiddley-om-pom-pom."
> So just let me be beside the seaside,
> I'll be beside myself with glee;
> And there's lots of girls beside, I should like to be beside,
> Beside the seaside, beside the sea!'

Sheridan's strength lay in his uplifting style and memorable songs which bridged the war years. During the conflict he lifted morale with his old numbers, and introduced equally successful patriotic songs, such as *Belgium Put The Kybosh On The Kaiser* (which made up in bounce what it lacked in historical truth). He even made the transition from straight Variety by appearing in *Gay Paree* at the Glasgow Coliseum. The year was 1918, and it was the start of his first long run in peace time; but audiences who sang and clapped along to his songs did not realize how much Sheridan had changed. The war and its unprecedented mass carnage had had a deep and lasting effect on him. His work-ing future looked assured, but in recurring bouts of depression the comic became convinced that his career was going into decline, and that people did not like him any more. After an enthusiastic reception at the Coliseum, he left the theatre and walked into Kelvin Grove Park, where he shot himself with a service revolver.

To achieve public acclaim, only to die violently was unusual; the chirpy stage presence demanded by Variety took a greater toll on comedians than perhaps any other performers. A few retired gracefully to rooms crammed with posters, photographs and mementoes, while others adjusted to empty days of oblivion, ill health or bankruptcy. Fame for many was an uphill struggle to escape terraced streets hemmed in by mills and factories. Those left behind followed their progress with wistful pride and, human nature being the way it is, a tinge of jealousy was inevitable.

Harry Fragson was an oddity even in the surreal world of Variety; he was an East Ender with a thick Cockney accent who spoke fluent French and became a star on both sides of the Channel. His father Victor was Belgian, and at home the family mostly spoke French, giving Harry – christened Leon Vince Philip Pott – the opportunity to sing in Paris pavement cafés at the age of seventeen. The bohemian atmosphere of the *cafés-chantants* encouraged him to write his own songs, and he was soon starring at the Folies-Bergère, where impresario Arthur Collins came across him. He, understandably, found it difficult to believe that the bright, pushy young French comedy singer was a Cockney, and booked him for his 1905 Drury Lane pantomime, *Cinderella*. It was Collins, incidentally, who set the pattern of casting variety stars in panto to pull in the crowds – a trend which still continues, with mixed results.

His Christmas shows were the most successful in the West End, and proved the perfect launch-pad for Fragson's career. He had been a big name in Paris for almost ten years, and was set for top billing in Britain. The melancholy-looking man, whose catch-phrase was 'Oh dear, I feel so queer,' was a complex character. London manager Chance Newton, who knew him well, described him as 'a delightful companion and a very kindly fellow,' but others saw him differently. William Boardman, who had managed both the Paris Alhambra and Brighton Hippodrome, knew him equally well and glimpsed something disturbing beneath the stage persona.

'There was something inscrutable, and at the same time magnetic in Fragson's personality,' he observed, 'something which drew as well as repelled. He was horribly alert, watchful, self-possessed. His restless, eager eyes seemed to be everywhere, his hard, unwinking gaze on everyone. There was something mocking in the way in which he proclaimed himself "your most humble and obedient servant." There was irony in the perfunctory bow and inquiring glance with which he greeted you when he strode out from the wings. There was defiance in the voice as he darted to the piano . . .'

Fragson's ageing father had moved out of London to the more familiar environment of Paris, where he looked after his son's apartment on Rue Lafayette, near Montmartre. He was said to be insanely jealous of his son's success, and increasingly befuddled by senility; if there was ever another side to the story, it was never recorded. Fragson, whose most famous number was *Hello, Hello, Who's Your Lady Friend*, had become engaged to a French dancer, Paulette Frank. He spent Christmas 1913 at Brighton finishing a show, and left to celebrate the new year in Paris with his fiancée. Soon after walking into his apartment a furious row erupted with his father, who pulled a gun and blew his son's brains out. More than 20,000 mourners attended the funeral at nearby Montmartre Cemetery, while the old man was commit-

Tommy Beamish with a French maid.

ted to an asylum. Harry Fragson was forty-four and worshipped by his followers; the true story of his tormented life off-stage, beset by family squabbles, will probably never be known.

ONE OF THE unbreakable commandments of Variety was the old tradition that the show must go on. There are legendary tales of performers going on against medical advice, reluctant to let down audiences who had queued to see them. Houdini, as we have seen, braved his final show with a burst appendix; and tragic, too, were those who soldiered on with long-term disabilities which would have hospitalized lesser men. It was an indication of the toughness and grit of variety performers, especially comedians, who had to summon the jollity to conceal their discomfort.

Dan Rolyat (his real name was Taylor, but he thought it looked more attractive spelled backwards) fell from a horse during a show in Newcastle in 1911, breaking his back. He recovered enough to make a successful come-back, despite constant pain. Rolyat's career was finally forced to a close when he was found to have cancer of the tongue, and he died in poverty.

Others managed bravely to capitalize on their infirmities. Billy Bennett's first night in his famous evening suit, for instance, had all the makings of a disaster. On his way from the dressing room to the wings he fell and seriously injured his ankle, and with only seconds to go before curtain-up, there was no time for first aid. He grimaced through his monologues and limped off feeling dreadful. The manager congratulated him on his facial expressions and suggested that he should keep them in the act.

George Formby Senior, whose son developed a toothy grin and a taste for cheeky songs, made a chesty cough his trademark – though few of his audience knew that, in the dressing room, the coughing did not stop. Variety girls recall with disgust how he used to support himself against the wall, hacking and spitting, after walking off. 'I'm coughing well toneet,' was his catchphrase, which made his working audiences roar, but it was slowly killing him.

He spent his early life in Wigan, and told jokes and stories in a dialect which northerners found a delight. George was born James Booth, in Ashton-under-Lyne, and took his stage name from railway sand wagons which rattled past his home bearing their town of origin – Formby – in big letters on the side. He was sent to work at twelve as a blacksmith's lad in a local iron foundry, where sulphur fumes from the coke fires permanently affected his lungs. Industrial safety was almost non-existent in heavy industry, and George became one of the many thousands of walking casualties of the mills and mines. He married Eliza

Hoy and moved in with his in-laws in Wigan, commuting by tram each night for a thirty shillings (£1.50) a week regular spot at the People's Palace in nearby St Helens.

Formby Senior was a quiet, thoughtful man, pallid from his chest complaint, and rarely without a cigarette in his hand. He dressed on stage in a tight-fitting coat, a tiny blocker jammed on his head and oversized boots on the wrong feet. With the possible exception of Frank Randle, a wild Northern comedian popular half a century later, Formby was one of the few comics who could raise a laugh simply by poking a foot from the wings. Audiences loved him, but surprisingly few recognized him off-stage. He chose to make himself up in the manner of an Edwardian actor rather than a comedian – number five flesh-coloured greasepaint and powder instead of white-face, and blue and red lines in the creases of his moon face. Above each eye he painted a dot to emphasize his features for the benefit of those up in the high galleries.

Eliza helped him develop his act by sitting out front and making notes, a role she was to later repeat for young George; she also suggested the first line of all his songs to nudge his inspiration. They usually followed the same theme – the naïve, wistful lad, bewildered by girls and city lights, and bossed around by his wife. George and Eliza ran the act like a business, making meticulous notes of bookings and expenses, keeping accounts and working into the early hours together on songs designed to raise a laugh among the ordinary people they had grown up with. One of his most famous, *Standing On The Corner Of The Street*, became an inspiration for their son George's *Leaning On A Lamp-post*. George Junior, incidentally, never saw his father perform, but studied his act from gramophone records. Formby Senior once shared digs with Edison and Bell, with whom he became friends, and was one of the first artists to make records.

Marie Lloyd, who met him in 'panto' and became a close friend of the family, said that there were only two comedians she would watch from the wings – Dan Leno and Formby Senior. His cough, which showed no sign of improvement, became increasingly difficult to control, so George incorporated it into the act. He and Eliza created a character, gormless John Willie, who had a bronchial cough, and the spot became one of his most popular. John Willie visited London with his down-to-earth wife, gaping in wonder at the street girls and art gallery nudes, until she dragged him away at the end of each chorus with the warning: 'John Willie – *come on!*' Formby would stop in the middle of the song to cough, remarking to the orchestra leader: 'Coughin' summat champion toneet!' He created Music Hall's biggest joke, Wigan Pier, which inspired the title of Orwell's book in 1937, and was responsible for an image which the council PR department is still working hard to rectify.

Formby sang his songs in a cracked, lugubrious voice which earned him the epiphet The Wigan Nightingale. Some of his funniest exhibited a sort of pathetic defiance at authority, defending the working man's right to a good time for no other reason than the fact that he deserved it. The sentiment appealed to his Northern audiences of 1910:

> Playing the game in the West,
> Leading a life that's thrilling.
> Out of the two-bob piece
> All I've got left is a shilling.
> Strolling along the Strand
> Knocking policemen about,
> And I'm not going home till a quarter to
>     ten
> 'Cause it's my night out.

By the end of the war he was earning £300 a week, with the distinction of being one of the first Northern dialect comedians to appeal to London audiences. He could not, however, bring himself to move permanently south and, with the help of a £1000 bonus from Moss Empires, bought a terraced house in Stockton Heath, Warrington, which became his base for touring the country. In 1921, while performing his celebrated coughing routine, he became unable to control his chest spasms. Formby collapsed with a burst blood vessel during the closing run of a pantomime at the Empire, Newcastle, and was taken home to Warrington, where he died on 8 February. He had built his whole career around his cough in order to conquer it, but it beat him in the end.

GEORGE FORMBY Senior's soulful talent placed him, as Marie Lloyd observed, alongside the great Dan Leno – another talented comedian who suffered greatly in the arduous cause of making people laugh. Leno, a supple little man of 1.6 km (5 ft 3 in), with a mobile, expressive face and, as someone once said, 'the eyes of a wounded animal', was a genius who inspired generations of stand-up comics. 'So little and frail a lantern,' said Max Beerbohm, 'could not long harbour so big a flame.' Beneath the arched eyebrows and wide mouth, always stretched in a half smile, lay a sensitive man who had a driving urge to be taken seriously. It has been the fatal flaw of many comedians, and few have achieved honest recognition outside their field. It pursued Leno like a mad dog and, together with the strain of work and business problems, resulted in a series of mental breakdowns which finally killed him in 1904 at the age of forty-three.

Only Chaplin conveyed the same impression of the tragedian lurking behind the comedian. Significantly, Dan's daughter, Georgina Leno Bruce, presented Charlie with the clogs her father wore in his

Dan Leno as the 'distinguished shop-walker.'

Drury Lane pantomimes with the note: 'No one has hitherto seemed to me worthy of wearing them . . .'

Leno did not really tell gags, but sang monologues while acting a range of characters from soldiers and washerwomen, to shop assistants, beefeaters and railway guards. He endeared himself to those who saw him because he always seemed to be baring his soul, imparting secrets and pieces of gossip. Despite the vastness of the theatres, his style was personal, intimate and reinforced with facial expressions which summed up his characters perfectly.

His parents, Mr and Mrs Johnny Wild – Singing And Acting Duettists – lived in St Pancras, where Leno was born George Galvin. He was thrust into a stage career at the age of two, in red and blue tights made from his mother's stockings, and a dancing suit run up from the stripes of a silk umbrella. As Little George The Infant Wonder And Posturer, he was easier to look after than being left in theatrical digs where, as a baby, he had slept in a drawer when his parents were working. When his father died, Leno's mother married a music hall singer who used the stage name Leno. George and his brother Jack liked the name and were soon hoofing in a double act called The Great Little Lenos.

He went solo as Dan Patrick Leno, Irish Character Vocalist, and even toured Ireland, where he picked up the slightest trace of a brogue which he kept for the rest of his life. Surprisingly, it was the obscure Northern passion of clog dancing which gave his career the biggest boost. He entered a competition for fun at a free-and-easy in Wakefield – deep in the heart of Yorkshire pie and peas country – and won a shoulder of mutton. The clatter of clog-irons on cobbles thundered like drums down the steep streets of mining and mill towns before the turn of the century. Clog dancing on bar floorboards and flagstones of pubs and clubs was immensely popular, and the most nimble-footed had their own soft-leather dancing clogs specially made in tooled hide, with decorated tongues. Leno, encouraged by his success, took part in a publicity stunt at the Princess's Palace, Leeds, to supposedly find The Champion Clog Dancer Of The World. 'The World' at that time did not stretch far beyond the suburbs of Headingley, but there was no shortage of competitors. The real purpose of the event was to attract crowds to watch two local clog dancers slog it out for supremacy. The gold and silver Lonsdale-style belt, worth £50, waited tantalizingly on stage. Leno, almost unknown, astonished everyone by winning the trophy outright.

Offers of work poured in and Dan, who had married a singer, Lydia Reynolds, during his stay in Leeds, found himself travelling all over the North. When he took his act to London, however, it was almost a disaster. Clog dancing was as alien as the watutsi, and only a few hands of polite applause echoed through Forester's Music Hall, in Mile End. Worried, he followed up

with a character song, *When Rafferty Raffled His Watch*, which to his relief brought the house down:

> The tables and chairs were tumbled
>   downstairs,
> We'd plenty of Irish and Scotch;
> And the divil's own fight there was on that
>   night,
> When Rafferty raffled his watch!

He needed little persuasion to drop the clog routine and concentrate on the songs.

Many writers, critics and devoted fans have tried to capture the vitality of his performance over the years, but the little man's stage presence eludes the written word, almost to the point of defying description. 'A diminutive figure with a mobile face, tragic eyes, the whole being of the man informed by a desperate earnestness, a fixed obsession to explain the unexplainable, to instruct the dullard and to carry the least imaginative and responsive member of his audience into the topsy-turvy world of mixed fact and wild fiction of which he was the chief inhabitant – does this convey anything of the magic?' J. B. Booth asked. 'He was patient – yet impatient. "Don't look so stupid," he would plead; and the house roared. Leno's humour was wild and inconsequent, yet at the same time, sane and keenly observed – an impossible paradox to anyone who never saw him . . .' Beerbohm summed it up more succinctly: . . . 'squirming in every limb with some deep grievance that must be outpoured, all hearts were his.'

Producers and promoters had enormous faith in Leno's ability to fill theatres. He was once approached by producer Milton Bode who wanted to book him for a provincial tour. When Leno explained that he was tied up with another contract, Bode offered him £125 a week for two years, with a down payment of £500 to persuade him to change his mind. 'You have all that faith in me?' Leno asked incredulously. 'All right, I accept. And don't bother about the deposit.' Halfway through the tour, when he was booked to appear in Sheffield, he received a request to perform at Sandringham before Edward VII. Leno went, worrying about letting down his Yorkshire audiences, and overwhelmed at the honour.

When he had finished his stage act in the quiet surroundings of the royal drawing room, Leno retired to his dressing room to change. He was removing his make-up when a footman appeared with a message that the King wished to see him in his smoking room. Leno scrambled to change into his dress suit, but could not find his trousers. Frantic rummaging through his theatrical trunk drew a blank, and with mounting anxiety he faced the prospect of a Royal audience in a dinner jacket and loud fawn check trousers. Finally his dresser, an enormously fat man, took off his own subdued blue serge trousers and offered them to his employer. Leno then discovered that his tie was also missing and had to borrow his obliging dresser's. Leaving his trusty servant in shirt tails, he went nervously to meet the King, trousers clamped at the back with safety pins, and tie wrapped three times round his neck to achieve a length more suited to his size. King Edward, delighted with the show, presented him with a diamond cravat pin bearing the Royal crest. Leno, from that moment on, was nicknamed the King's Jester by his followers.

The tiny comedian shared a trait of secret generosity with his friend Marie Lloyd. In the last few years of his life he visited the threadbare taverns off the Strand late at night, giving money to anyone with a hard-luck story – usually in sums out of all proportion to their needs. When he died he left £10,000, but is thought to have given away many times that amount.

Throughout his career he had always seen himself as a Shakespearean actor, performing either Hamlet or Richard III. It became an obsession; in private he dressed in character and went as far as to learn both entire parts in case he should ever be made an offer at short notice. As he realized just how slim that possibility was, Leno desperately set about putting together his own Shakespearean production.

Constance Collier, a Gaiety Girl and outstanding Edwardian beauty, arrived home in the small hours in 1903 for a late supper with her mother. When their brougham pulled up outside her apartment in Shaftesbury Avenue, near Seven Dials, the two women paid the driver and noticed another cab waiting outside the door. Inside the house they glanced into the darkened sitting room to encounter Dan Leno sitting on the sofa in the moonlight. Later, they learned from the maid that he had been waiting for three hours.

Constance Collier put on the light and sat beside the comedian, whom she recognized but had never met. For half an hour he told her his life story, holding her hand tightly. When he felt he could broach the purpose of his visit, Leno confessed that his dearest ambition was to play Shakespeare; he had the capital to subsidize a production – would she sign a five year contract to play opposite him?

Miss Collier could hardly take him seriously. The proposition would have meant abandoning a promising West End career with the actor-manager Beerbohm Tree. To lever herself from an embarrassing situation she tactfully, if rather weakly, suggested that he should talk it over with Tree the following morning. Leno, unaware that he had been rejected, left in a state of high enthusiasm.

A few hours later, with hardly any time for sleep, he was already waiting at His Majesty's Theatre before the cast arrived for rehearsals. When Tree walked in, looking slightly puzzled at Leno's presence, they sat down together in the stalls and fell into deep conversation. Tree appeared fascinated and deeply interested but was, in fact, agreeing with everything Leno said in order to get rid of him. He either lacked the courage to give an honest opinion, or was so contemptuous of Leno's wild scheme that he was playing games with him – probably a little of both. The comedian left after an hour, and when Constance Collier arrived home, he was waiting for her in the drawing room with a small parcel and a sheaf of papers. After the events of the previous twenty-four hours she was somewhat startled to see him, and a little angry that Tree had lobbed the ball neatly back into her court in so ungentlemanly a fashion. Leno with his hair parted in the centre and plastered down, handed her an expensive diamond encrusted wall plaque – and the contract. Constance, as gently as possible, handed them back, and Leno left in tears.

The rejection pushed him to breaking point. For more than forty years, since the age of two, he had appeared almost nightly on stage – a tremendous strain for anyone – staying up through the small hours in later years to listen to the problems of the poor in smokey ale-houses. His nerves were also stretched with pressure piled on him by powerful theatre owners who were trying to close down his business interests.

Leno, disenchanted with theatre managers, had gone into partnership with three other comedians – Herbert Campbell who starred with him in Drury Lane 'pantos', Harry Randall and Fred Williams – to run their own theatres. In 1898, they bought a modest 500-seat hall in Clapham Junction, and later acquired another in Croydon. But having played the finest theatres in Britain, they had nurtured an urge to have one built to their own design. They found the ideal site at Walham Green, where Fulham Broadway now runs. Frank Matcham, the theatre architect, was commissioned to create a 1,500-seat theatre called the Granville. It turned out to be a magnificent building, sadly demolished in 1971, with blue and gold plasterwork and Doulton china decorations.

The quartet of comedians were delighted with the result, but theatre-chain proprietors saw it only as threatening competition, and piled the pressure on Leno to pull out. The three theatres flourished until the syndicates smarting at their success, launched a ruthless war against them until they were forced out of business and lost their entire investment.

The disaster took a heavy toll; Leno suffered a nervous breakdown and was admitted to a private mental hospital. Months later he allowed himself to be coaxed back to take part in the Drury Lane pantomime in which he had appeared for fifteen consecutive years. The fee was £250 a week, but Leno was a walking shadow. His heart seemed no longer in the business and his rubber face was pale and emaciated. 'They'll have to call me L-e-a-n-o now,' he half joked to his dresser as he studied himself in the mirror.

On opening night he had difficulty remembering his lines, and Harry Randall, working opposite him, had to constantly feed him prompts. The audience rustled restlessly with embarrassment. His comic antics, which had made him a legend, seemed strangely wooden and contrived. The applause was polite, more out of respect for a fallen hero.

Campbell, his other Granville partner, had also suffered ill health since the collapse of the business. For the finale he joined Leno on stage for the traditional refrain:

> We hope to appear
> For many a year
> In the panto at old Drury Lane.

Neither of them did – Campbell died from a heart attack a few months later; Dan Leno struggled on making appearances, but suffered another mental breakdown from which he never recovered. He died a few days after it in 1904. The only way to assess anyone's stature, a friend once told him, is to look at the size of the monument they erect when he is dead. An unreliable theory, of course, but on the site of the house where Dan Leno grew up they built St Pancras station.

IN THE LATE 1800s an actor, detecting a familiar sound deep in the auditorium, would whisper to his colleague from the side of his mouth: 'The bird's there.' The hiss would grow so deafening, like a gaggle of angry geese, that a play could be brought to a halt in the middle of a scene. Getting the bird evolved into a riskier business in the uninhibited atmosphere of Variety, when artists were driven from the stage fending off a storm of missiles.

It was a baptism even the most famous performers went through as they learned their craft by trial and error. Audiences expected a certain standard of artistry which, though difficult to articulate, was understood to a fine degree. It amounted to an assessment of talent and an appreciation of genius which each member of the working class audience could instinctively define; and artists who failed to give their money's worth had to suffer the consequences.

Audiences, as many stars readily acknowledged, created success; they recognized when they were in the presence of a great performer and noisily acknowledged it. The big names of Variety felt flattered to receive high praise and critical acclaim from the world of arts and letters, but they knew in their hearts that it came only because the raggle taggle army in the gods had decreed it first.

George Robey, knighted in later life, was one of the many who paid tribute to the audiences who made him a star. 'Yours truly has been top of the bill during the reign of five monarchs,' he said in 1937. 'Forty-seven years – that's how long I've been a laughable object, at least in public.

That's a world record of which I am very proud, and I hope you are too. For it's you who made me what I am.'

Ganga Dun, Priestley's stage magician in *Lost Empires* had contempt for the intellect of his audiences, but he knew he had to court them, humour them and metaphorically jest and tumble to remain top of the bill. Robey felt so indebted to his fans that he went on to pen an ingratiating verse to them:

> . . . Of course there are moments when
> trifles go wrong;
> An artist's life isn't all clover,
> But you've had a part in these milestones of
> song
> For you've helped me in putting them
> over.
> And every time I achieve a success
> The laughter rings merry and bright,
> I take off my hat and say, 'Well, that's that;
> I think I shall sleep well tonight.'

Audiences were tolerant with old favourites whose standards temporarily slipped, but newcomers could find themselves facing a hostile reception. Rough and ready variety-goers expected to be treated with the respect due to paying customers, and even the most harmless banter could turn ugly if handled arrogantly. A typical Edwardian encounter, reported in the Midlands, began with a comedian singing very badly and laughing too loudly at his own jokes. In due course a voice from the gallery bellowed good-humouredly: 'If tha can't do better than that – get off the bloody stage!' There were guffaws from the audience, who were prepared to give the comic a chance, until he replied: 'Ah! That's what I like to see – a bit of local humour. Now, as I was saying . . .' He had made the fatal mistake of insulting them, and the atmosphere rapidly cooled. The lone voice in the gallery was now speaking for everyone: 'If tha doesn't get off that stage, tha'll get some bloody carrots and tatas for nowt!'

The comedian wisely began to edge towards the wings and the crowd, sensing his lack of authority (or cowardice, if you prefer) pelted the stage with rotten vegetables. Many used to take bags of over-ripe fruit in readiness; Irish eggs, well past the Edwardian equivalent of the sell-by date, were available at fifty for a shilling (5p) from shops which conveniently stayed open late near the theatre – too conveniently, some artists felt.

MOST AUDIENCES had discriminating taste, but the nicest people could find themselves on the receiving end. Little Tich, one of the most loved, and lovable, stars of Variety made an uncomfortable tour of Australia in 1927. In the home of dwarf-throwing they failed to appreciate his simple humour, and tossed showers of pennies on the stage of the Tivoli, Melbourne. Similar treatment had been handed out the week before, but Tich stood his ground. He pulled himself up to his full height and told them that they had just delivered what his profession regarded as the greatest possible insult. Then he walked straight off to the manager's office and terminated his contract.

It showed remarkable courage for a man who had fought physical disability to become one of the biggest names in Variety. Back in Britain, Little Tich was fondly regarded as one of the funniest comedians on the halls. He took his name from the Tichborne Claimant, Arthur Orton, who became a music hall attraction after his release from prison on fraud charges. Originally, Tich was billed as The Great Little Mackney, until burnt-cork singer E. W. Mackney (The Great Mackney, Negro Delineator) found out and forced him to change his name. The pint-size comedian took it philosophically: 'There's already a Big Tich,' he shrugged, referring to 127 kg (20 st) Orton, 'Why not a little one?'

Little Tich began his career when Music Hall was fading, and his act brought nostalgic memories of distant delights to the new Variety shows. He was an extremely agile dancer, which was quite an achievement, if the stories were true, for someone with two extra toes on each foot and five fingers and a thumb on each hand. Tich was said to be very sensitive about his deformity, and generally wore gloves on stage. He was certainly touchy about his height which, although never accurately published, is said to have been little more than that of a ten-year-old child.

In private, Little Tich, born Harry Relph, was a cultured, intelligent man – a

Little Tich.

proficient cellist; a linguist fluent in French, German, Italian and Spanish; and a dedicated philosophy student. All of which was difficult to imagine for those who saw his stage act.

'He has hardly reached the centre of the stage and begun rattling away at some song that is only meant to be half-heard before you are tickled,' J. B. Priestley wrote for the *Daily Telegraph* in 1925. 'His songs are nothing. But his antics, his sudden gestures, are astounding. He will tell you, in a kind of drolly indignant tone, how he went in or came out of somewhere or other, and then he will illustrate it with such verve that his tiny legs seem to vibrate rather than to move as ordinary legs move. His feet go pitter-patter-pit; he assumes a ridiculous attitude; then cocks a knowing, droll eye, taking the whole assembly into his confidence; and you, like all the rest, are won over at a bound.'

His fluency in French made him a big star in Paris where, in recognition of his talent, he was made an officer of the *Academie Francaise*. Tich, who could balance on the toes of his two-foot long dancing shoes, privately had a greater fondness for ballet than knockabout hoofing. He married a Spanish prima ballerina in Paris, and when she died in 1926 became engaged to Ivy Latimer, a British actress. Tich guarded his privacy and went to great lengths to keep the wedding ceremony quiet. He took elaborate precautions to avoid publicity at St Giles register office, Bloomsbury, by announcing that the wedding had been postponed. Nothing, it seemed, could keep the crowds of his admirers away. They camped outside the doors all Saturday afternoon, leaving only when the registrar had locked up and gone home. An hour later, by special arrangement, he returned with Tich and Ivy to conduct the ceremony.

As seriously as he took his private life, he conducted his stage act in a curious way, always seeming detached from it and slightly tongue in cheek. 'He had a supreme artistic gift for approaching the subject obliquely,' said Edwardian critic Archibald Haddon. 'In every character he conveyed the quintessence of grotesquerie – as Johnnie green, performing ludicrous antics with cap and cane; as a blacksmith with a hammer almost as large as himself; a garrulous butcher's boy getting tied up in a string of sausages; a Jack tar parodying the Hornpipe; or the Duchess of Devonshire Cream, posing in a gilt frame *à la* Gainsborough. In each instance he would be well outside the part, yet monumentally effective, in spite of his lack of inches, for he was only 4 ft 6 in or thereabouts.'

Priestley noticed his odd detachment, too: 'He stands away from his jokes, merely proffering them with a wink and a grin. The comic thing is not that he should really be doing them, but that he should be pretending to do them. He does not act out a man telling you something funny about his mother-in-law, but a man pretending to be a man telling you about his mother-in-law. The unsophisticated enjoy his obvious drolleries; the sophisticated enjoy his winks and shrugs and comic asides. When he drops his hat and finds that he cannot pick it up because he always kicks it, you may or may not laugh; but when having done this once or twice, he says: 'Comic business with *chapeau*,' there is something wrong with you if you do not laugh. Thus he is greater than the tradition, and remains with us at once a legend and a personality.'

Few elevated comedy to such a fine art, and perhaps even fewer managed to keep their feet so firmly on the ground. Tich was unimpressed with the trappings of stardom and always kept his stage career in perspective. He showed great concern about the most feudal relationship between theatre managers and their artists, and was one of the founder members of the Variety Artists' Federation. In 1903, he played a leading part in a strike which closed down twenty-five London theatres, picketing as many of them as his time would allow.

His devotion to the Federation was partly a personal reaction to cost-conscious managements and changing times. 'Those were the days,' he said wistfully of Music Hall. 'I put in seventeen years at the dear old Tivoli. One engagement there lasted twenty-two months. I would stroll quietly down to the hall after dinner and just enter into the fun of the thing – like a happy-go-lucky, jolly *soirée*. Now we have to slave from two till eleven – three performances daily – eighteen a week . . .'

There was always an innocence about his act but, perhaps because of his size and inoffensive nature, he was singled out for attack when Variety met with conservative disapproval. Music Hall of the late 1800s, with its saucy songs, attendant beer-swilling and bawdy behaviour, precipitated a small but influential puritan backlash. It had been bubbling under for some time, until Marie Lloyd's song, *A Saucy Bit O'Crackling*, opened a floodgate. For reasons no one fully understood, Little Tich's harmless sketches became a focus of vigorous complaint. He was, as William Archer wrote at the time, 'thrown to the wolves of criticism.' Tich's loyal audiences, interpreting it as an attack on their own lifestyle, closed ranks and ensured that his popularity was unaffected. Tich, sensitive to the onslaught, bounced back in *Lord Tom Noddy* at the Garrick, before taking the show on the road for four successful seasons. The little man who began his career playing the tin whistle and dancing on cellar flaps in Gravesend, was clearly one of their own.

In the old days, audiences had encouraged performers to stick to their favourite songs and sketches; Variety with its constant striving for new material, lived up to its name. But strangely, pre-World War I audiences still clamoured for Tich's old act. Wherever he appeared he was greeted with a rising chorus of 'Boots! Boots!' as they begged for his long-shoe dance.

The spot proved too exhausting as he became older and, after a bad fall on a sloping stage, he abandoned his famous trademark. Years later, in 1922, he reappeared without warning wearing the celebrated boots at the Coliseum – slapping his feet and standing on his toes as though the clock had been turned back twenty years. After that single performance he packed them away and they were never seen again.

Tich came from the common people and they took him to their heart. George Robey, their other great hero, could hardly have had a background more removed from his homespun audiences, or indeed, his fellow performers. He came from a middle class family from Herne Hill, and was educated at Leipzig University and Cambridge, where he took a science degree. Robey worked as an engineer for four years before becoming a comedian, and throughout his life cultivated tastes and interests of which his audiences were seldom aware. He became an expert on British poetry; exhibited paintings at the Royal Academy; was acknowledged as one of the country's leading violin makers and restorers; acquired a formidable knowledge of Egyptology and Assyriology; and spent hours listening to Wagner. In the evenings he went to work, put on the greasepaint and earned up to £600 a week with his earthy jokes. 'I believe in honest vulgarity,' he used to say. 'There is nothing in this world so good as a full-throated laugh. It keeps us from brooding over matters of sex.'

Robey's humour was Elizabethan, forcefully delivered in a semi-clerical frockcoat and flat bowler, with a florid twirl of his famous brown cane. He had horseshoe eyebrows which shot up in indignant reproof when they laughed at his innuendoes. And when they laughed until they could not stop he would boom in mock anger: 'Desist! Temper your hilarity with a modicum of reserve. I beg you. Consider my position. This is no time for airy persiflage . . .'

Robey's fruity, erudite commands held his working class audiences spellbound – only to collapse in giggles a second later because they did not understand a word. On and on he drove them with his cane, like a tireless herdsman or a mad schoolmaster, whipping up peals of laughter at some suggestive remark, only to slap them down again for daring to laugh. When the whole house was rolling in the aisle he would raise his voice in distaste. 'I know that you have parted with a small portion of largesse in return for a modicum of clean, wholesome fun. But I see no *reason* for this *unseemly* mirth!' Then, at the height of his diatribe he would belch alcoholically

and say in a very correct Home Counties voice: 'Pardon – but we had a very *rich* tea.' Audiences had seen all the 'toff' comedians of the 'broken-down swell' variety in their day. But here, apparently, was a real gentleman comedian; one of Them, yet one of Us. He stood with authority in the centre of the stage, shouting orders, admonishing, insulting and constantly telling them to 'Shurrup!' as they laughed until they ached.

There was no doubt that he was an intuitive comic genius with a gift for the spontaneous aside, but every detail of his appearance had been carefully planned. The red nose, check suit and baggy trousers were never part of Robey's make-up. 'In my young days,' he said, 'I spent a lot of time and thought evolving all sorts of

George Robey.

comic make-ups. It nearly turned my hair grey trying to think out costumes that would be funnier and more absurd than anything I had worn before. Suddenly I got an idea. Why have different costumes – why not always have the same one? Then people would get to know my appearance.

'The problem was to think out something good. I knew all humour depended on contrast, so I studied my face in the mirror and tried to think out the costume that would make it look funniest. Now when a man is on the stage, the parts of him that catch the attention of the audience most are his teeth and the whites of his eyes. However, I didn't want to black my face to draw attention to my eyes, so I exaggerated my naturally bushy eyebrows.

'The teeth were more difficult to manage for I soon discovered that a white collar was too conspicuous, and that if I wore one, my teeth would not be very noticeable. So I decided that I wouldn't wear a collar. To give myself an air of dignity, which would contrast with my comic appearance, I decided on a black frock coat. In its normal state it made me look like a parson, so I cut the collar off that as well. I completed the costume with a tiny little bowler hat – again the contrast between a big head and a small hat – and decided that I would do.' Robey also observed that he had unusually large spacing between his eyebrows and eyelids, and made use of the fact by practising exaggerated eyebrow movements. With others, such a studied approach might have proved their undoing, but Robey had the advantage of also being a natural.

Of his humour he admitted: 'I've cracked some saucy ones in my time, but I've always tried to be modest in my vulgarity. I have never said a thing I would not say in front of a family.' On balance it was probably true – Robey's simple humour gave audiences the cue to let their imaginations run wild.

His career, which begun at the Horns Assembly Rooms, Kennington, in 1891 and continued almost to his death at the age of eighty-five, spanned the transition from Music Hall to Variety. 'Comedy,' he maintained, 'hasn't changed a jot. The foundations of humour are as old as the world. Fashions in everything else may change with the centuries and the eras – but the things which make people laugh, real, honest-to-goodness laughter, I mean – have never changed. And they never will . . .'

His songs, like those of any variety artist of the day, played an essential part in knitting his act together. Robey stuck to the ones his audience shouted loudest for – 'If you want to be happy you must never try to be a reformer,' he said of them. The bowler was introduced for the first time at the Star music hall, Bermondsey, with the song *My Hat's A Brown 'Un*. It had such an effect that the audience continued to sing it through every act for the rest of the programme. The furious manager flatly refused to allow Robey to appear there again.

Even his early numbers – *The Simple Pimple* and *He'll Get It Where He's Gone To Now* – remained favourites for years. But the one they requested again and again was *If You Were The Only Girl In The World*, which earned him £500 a week in *The Bing Boys*, a World War I Alhambra revue which filled the stalls with khaki and had everyone joining in. Requests for the song haunted him throughout his life, from command performances to charity nights. George always obliged, though later in life he admitted that he hated it: 'Of all the maudlin sentimental trash, that's just the worst in the world. I hate it. I loathe it. Wherever I go, if it's a benefit, if I open a bazaar in Canada, South Africa, everywhere; as soon as a band sees George Robey it starts playing that tune.'

*The Bing Boys* successfully eased Robey over the watershed created by the war years, which marked a change in emphasis

George Robey.

from Variety to revue. The show, which opened in 1916 ran for nine months and was seen by more than 600,000 people, boosting his popularity and broadening his career. The following year he organized a concert for the French Red Cross which brought in £11,265; by the end of the war he had raised half a million pounds for the Red Cross and was awarded the C.B.E. Robey went on to star in revue, radio shows, films, Shakespearean productions and, at the age of sixty-two, turned to operetta.

Few artists adapted so well to the changing years. Perhaps equally remarkable was the fact that Robey entered the business quite by chance. As a young engineer watching a show at the Westminster Aquarium he volunteered to be hypnotized by a mesmerist, Professor Tom Kennedy. The willing subject failed to go into a trance, but kept up such an hilarious pretence that he was asked to join the act. Robey worked unpaid, but was soon offered a spot of his own by the Aquarium management. He was knighted in 1954 and died a few months later at home in Saltdean, Sussex, clutching his little brown cane.

Variety, by that time, was almost dead. The great Edwardian theatres limped through the lack-lustre 1950s staging strip shows to fight the growing appeal of bingo and television. The theatre revolution, the boom in high street cinemas and the huge appeal of radio had eroded its spirit by providing the public with a wider, more sophisticated choice of popular entertainment.

As the pace of life accelerated up to the brink of war in 1914, quick-fire variety shows – disposing of Music Hall's master of ceremonies and intervals between turns – had created the mould for the future. By degrees, programmes were telescoped into a single show of non-stop revue. Radio light entertainment removed, overnight, the need for comedians to look funny – eccentric suits, funny hats, red noses and twirling canes became no match for an endless stream of gags. The swagger, the wink and the raised eyebrow – all the ingredients of what Robey called 'good, honest English vulgarity' – became the flotsam and jetsam of the airwaves.

The frantic progress of peacetime brought new prosperity, too, blurring many of the old class distinctions. One of the first casualties was the strict social division of the theatre. 'The old dress circle was always the stupidest part of an audience,' James Agate believed. After all, he argued, they were responsible for branding some of the great comic geniuses 'low' comedians. 'The dress circle, lacking both the experience of the gallery and the imagination of the stalls, was not touched by all this patter of red noses, gin and mother-in-law. The dress circle knew nothing of these things and saw in them no 'criticism of life.' 'Today,' he wrote in 1924, 'our larger palaces of Variety are all dress circle, with a life impervious to shafts from the Music Hall.'

Billy Bennett, Dan Leno and Little Tich had spoken for the lower rungs of the social ladder; Marie Lloyd and Bessie Bellwood mirrored their innermost feelings; Albert Chevalier, Harry Champion and the coster singers told of life on the local street corner. But there was no one to speak up for commuters from the newly-built suburbs – yet their numbers were growing by the day. Poverty, pawn-shops, large families and leaking roofs did not feature prominently in the sprawling developments springing up where the Tube lines snaked out of the city. 'The artists who can get into the marrow of life as it is lived in Tooting have not yet arisen,' Agate wrote, 'and I very much doubt whether the Tootingites want them to arise.'

The grip of Variety slackened as life became more respectable and far removed from the East End back-to-backs where, 'wiv a ladder and some glasses you could see the 'Ackney Marshes – if it wasn't for the 'ouses in between.' But for some, in the words of coster comedian Gus Elen, who sang those lines, it was all 'a great big shame.'

# LOST EMPIRES, ALHAMBRAS & ✳ PALACES ✳

Theatre Royal, Nottingham.

IN 1889, at two in the morning, a policeman walking his beat along Brook Street, Holborn, was surprised to see the front door of number twenty flung open and a dishevelled man run down the steps into his arms. He was clearly in a state of excitement, pulling at the constable's tunic and half-dragging him into the house to show him something. In a dimly-lit, untidy room at the back the policeman saw, with growing amazement, moving pictures of people walking at Hyde Park Corner projected on the wall.

The unknown bobby had the distinction of being possibly the world's first cinema 'audience', while William Friese-Greene, the man who cranked the primitive projector, died without distinction, £20,000 in debt. His pioneering work in cinema-photography preceeded Edison, to whom Hollywood gave most of the credit, and laid the foundation for an invention which changed the face of public entertainment within twenty years.

The idea was not new; people had yearned for moving pictures for almost a century. As early as 1782, Gainsborough the painter built a 'show box' through which twelve-inch square painted land-scapes could be viewed. Sliding backdrops, moved to and fro, gave the impression of moonlight and dappled sunshine. Painting on glass was an art which Gainsborough had clearly not mastered – his efforts were crude and unsophisticated compared with those of the unknown craftsmen who created magic lantern slides half a century later. However, the effect was the important thing; Victorians were fascinated by the Zoetrope, a parlour game device which looked like a spinning cake tin with slits cut around the sides. A picture strip around the inside gave the impression of movement, making dolphins leap, cyclists pedal furiously and frogs hop up and down. Regent Street Polytechnic installed one in the foyer, next to its diving bell, in 1856.

Ideas to create moving pictures, kinematics as it became known, came thick and fast – Sir William Herschel the astronomer became fascinated by a dinner table trick of spinning a coin on a plate so that both head and tail could be seen simultaneously. He made a spinning disc – the Thaumatoscope – with a bird on one side and a cage on the other, so that the images fused together in motion. The Phenakistoscope and Strobo-scope followed, based on observations of Dr Roget (of Thesaurus fame) who noticed that moving wheels appeared stationary through the slats of a venetian blind. Then there was the Fantascope – a dial of moving pictures showing a wife beating her husband with a stick – and the Viviscope, which was almost identical, but portraying a negro eating a melon. The Praxinoscope used images reflected from mirrors on a wheel; the Filoscope, based on thumb-flick books, was the precursor of the What-The-Butler-Saw slot machines.

Movies came a step nearer with the Bio-Phantoscope, invented by J. A. R. Rudge of Bath in 1868. He developed a home-spun show called Life In The Lantern, which threw a series of photographic slides on to a screen in quick succession, giving the impression of a man taking his head off his body and tucking it under his arm. The body belonged to Rudge, the head was Friese-Greene's and the machine a promising mechanical forerunner of the movie projector.

ABOUT THE TIME Friese-Greene was filming at Hyde Park Corner, a French-born inventor, Louis Le Prince was filming with his own camera on a bridge in Leeds. His mechanic, James Langley, who helped him build the equipment, recalled the first pictures: '. . . the tram horses were seen moving over it, and all the other traffic, as if you was on the bridge yourself. I could even see the smoke coming out of a man's pipe who was lounging on the bridge.' Friese-Greene's pictures were of a slightly poorer quality, but he had made the breakthrough of punching sprocket-holes in the margin of the film to prevent it jumping from side to side in the projector. Soon after his experiments in Leeds, Le Prince, who was the son of a French army officer, disappeared in a mysterious fashion. He was last seen on 16 September 1890 boarding a train for Paris at Bourges; his luggage and business papers vanished along with him. Le Prince's widow always maintained that he had been abducted by rivals.

Celluloid roll film, introduced to Britain by Eastman in 1889, helped the early pioneers to make great strides. Previously, Friese-Greene had soaked ribbons of paper in castor oil to make them transparent. Remarkably, he filmed a Brighton street scene using this method on a camera which cost him £150 to build. He was not satisfied with the results and bought raw celluloid to work on. Friese-Greene softened it with the steam from thirty kettles scattered around his workroom, and passed it through the family mangle to roll it thinner before cutting into strips. With the finished film he showed an endless reel of a skeleton dancing in a Piccadilly shop window and caused a minor sensation. The jerky pictures were thrown on to a screen surrounded by brown paper, which concealed a small boy cranking the projector. The agitated crowd outside became so large that police had to be called to forcibly drag the boy (who was enjoying every minute) from the machine.

These early experiments mushroomed into a film industry completely dominated by shoestring British productions. The Bioscope, as it became known, was a great attraction on travelling fairgrounds, though not without some initial scepticism by the stall-holders. For years they had been giving magic lantern shows of a very high quality, which gave the illusion of movement. Early films were crude by comparison, and lacked the colour and definition of the lantern slides. Because the early reels were so short – some only ninety seconds long – it was impossible to put a substantial film show together. The first efforts needed a home and found it accompanying lantern slides or as a novelty at the end of variety shows. At first, some stage artists laughed and claimed that it was the quickest way of clearing the auditorium after the final curtain. Others had their doubts and saw in the flickering pictures a gloomy vision of the future.

The first Bioscope reels were crude and modest and sold for fourpence a foot. The public liked them and, from the showman's point of view, they could be screened by an unskilled operator while he attended to other business. Fairground barkers from all over Britain travelled to 'Flicker Alley' – Cecil Court, off Charing Cross Road – to buy from the distributors. It proved to be a profitable pilgrimage; soon a small operator could buy a complete programme for £5 which would bring in up to £300 a week in takings.

Lt-Col A. C. Bromhead, one of the founders of Gaumont, which began life in two small rooms in Cecil Court, dealt with the stream of fairground folk. One woman, he recalled, wanted to buy a £50 Chronos projector, which was a big investment at the time. 'She slowly explored her clothing,' he said, 'and finally produced a red stocking from under her petticoat. From that bright and unexpected article she counted out the payment – and took a long time to do it, for the whole sum was paid in threepenny-bits.'

Film catalogues from the 1890s featured shorts lasting only a minute or two each, with titles such as *How Briget Served The Salad Undressed*. This popular scenario, recycled many times, showed the dim but nubile Briget misunderstanding the salad order and delivering the meal in a state of *déshabillé*. Two hundred feet of film hardly allowed time to develop story lines. In *The Pretty Stenographer* an 'elderly but gay stockbroker' dictates a letter to his pretty typist, and stoops to steal a kiss as his wife walks in. The outraged woman twists her husband's ear until he falls to his knees, and the typist bursts into tears. End of performance.

Regent Street Polytechnic staged one of the first public shows on 20 February 1896, causing widespread panic with a shot of a train chugging into view, head-on to camera. No one, it seemed, could be persuaded that it would not carry on straight through the back of the theatre. The engine driver – undoubtedly the world's first screen hero – managed to pull up as the reel flickered to a close. The scene was included in a half-hour package supplied by the French Lumiere brothers, and had been screened in Paris two months earlier. The programme of twenty-five half-minute films, with an introduction between each while the operator changed the reel, moved on to the Empire music hall in Leicester Square and ran for eighteen months.

Elsewhere the Bioscope flourished to the sound of fairground organs, and in penny gaffs which sprang up throughout the East End. They were makeshift affairs – often old shops with their fittings hastily ripped out to cash in on the novelty of films. George Pearson, an early movie pioneer, recalled his first visit: 'It was a derelict greengrocer's shop. The hawk-eyed gentleman on a fruit crate was bewildering a sceptical crowd. In that shuttered shop was "a miracle to be seen for a penny," but only twenty-four could enter at a time. "You've seen pictures of people in books – all frozen stiff. You've never seen people coming alive in pictures, moving about all natural like you and me. Well, go inside and see for yourself. Then tell me if I'm a liar," the man declared. Inside was an all-pervading smell of rotten vegetables and dried mud. A furtive youth did things to a tin oven on legs, and a white sheet swung from the ceiling. We grouped around the oven and wondered. Suddenly someone turned down a gas jet and the tin apparatus burst into a fearful clatter. An oblong picture slapped onto the screen and began a dreadful dance. It turned out to be a picture of a house on fire. After exactly one minute the light went up, and I had seen my first cinema show.'

Many of the penny gaffs featured primitive music hall turns to make the programme longer. Local pubs were among the first to suffer as customers deserted the bar for the nightly show – but soon they began hitting back with their own attractions. George Augustus Sala in his *Papers, Humorous and Pathetic* saw the customer-war at first-hand in the 1890s: 'The gaff had been a shop, converted into a hall of delight by the very simple process of knocking down a partition between the shop and the parlour at the back. The gas fittings yet remain, and even the original counters, which are converted into "reserve seats", where for the outlay of twopence as many costers, thieves and young ladies as can fight for a place are sitting, standing and lounging . . . The place is abominably dirty, and the odour of the company generally, and the shag tobacco they were smoking is powerful . . . Silence for the manager, please! – who comes forward with an elaborate bow, and a white hat in his hand, to address the audience. A slight disturbance has occurred, it appears, in the course of the evening. The "impresario" complains bitterly of the "mackinations" of certain parties next door, who seek to injure him by creating an uproar . . . The next door parties are the proprietors of a public house who have sought to seduce away the supporters of the gaff by vaunting the superior qualities of their cream gin, a cuckoo clock, and the "longest cheroots in the world for a penny.'"

Robert Paul, an early film-maker, was impressed by the success of these early shows, and stepped up his output by producing the first British screen comedy. He borrowed three music hall artists from the Alhambra, where his films were showing, and carried some of the scenery on to the theatre roof. *The Soldier's Courtship*, which lasted less than two minutes, featured a canoodling private and a children's nanny being squeezed off a park bench by a fat lady reading a book. It was such a success that Paul followed with more comedies and news reel coverage of events of the day, maintaining a constantly changing programme at the Alhambra, which ran for two years. The Bioscope enjoyed a brief boom in variety theatres, with operators racing from hall to hall each night in horse-drawn cabs, carrying reels of film and cumbersome projection equipment. After a few years the novelty began to pale and, for a while, films receded to the fairground again. A great effort was made to establish them as family entertainment – some fairgrounds carried up to six tented Bioscope shows at a time, billing their wares as Moral And Refined, Pleasing To Ladies.

AS TECHNIQUES improved and programmes became longer, films began to ease themselves back into town halls and more permanent accommodation. By 1904, with the help of people like Gaumont's Lt-Col Broadhead, halls were converted into 'Kinemas'. Gaumont opened The Daily Bioscope, in Bishopsgate, which seated a hundred people. Henry Hibbert of Wardour Films, one of the first distributors, recalled the projection problems of the era: 'The great difficulty was the question of light. Electricity was in its infancy and there was no electric light, so we had to work with gas. We used oxygen under pressure in tubes, and hydrogen from the mains, but the density of film in those days was so irregular that we had great difficulty in getting the light through it all. The machines never had to be more than twelve to sixteen feet from the screen, there were no spool boxes, and we just had to run the films from the top spool through the gate, and let them finish in a basket, or on the floor. The lighting method was very hot and the films began to warp with the heat, and ultimately catch fire . . . Then electric light became common and we began to make use of it. From that point the development of modern machines was swift and logical.'

Films did not become universally popular until about 1907, when catalogues were offering programmes such as *The Great Train Robbery*, which lasted twenty minutes and showed robbers being chased for holding up a train. D. W. Griffith – later to make the first box office hit *The Birth of a Nation* – released *The Adventures of Dolly* which became a great attraction. A year later the Edwardians' ever-shifting hunger for new fads proved the answer to the film industry's prayer, when the great roller-skating bubble finally burst, leaving hundreds of empty rinks on the verge of bankruptcy. Many of these elaborate sheds were turned into plush cinemas, with seats in place of wooden benches, potted palms on each side of the screen and a pianist to enhance the atmosphere. An hour's viewing cost twopence and, for an extra penny, tea and biscuits were available. The first purpose-built cameras also began to appear and saved the frantic stampede to shift equipment from one theatre to the next.

By this time the choice of programmes was enormous, and film-makers were constantly hunting for new material. 'I found that the difficulty in those early days was to get subjects for films,' said pioneer Henry Hibbert. 'The first real business proposition that came my way was in 1901, at the time of the death of Queen Victoria. I was offered £50 if I could show a film of the funeral in Bradford on the night of the day on which it took place. I had hardly any money, but I went up to London with my camera, begged a place at the corner of a stand (I could not afford to pay for the privilege) and took my pictures. I developed some on my way back to Bradford, finished them at my lodgings, and for the same night they were shown in Forster Square.

'After this I went to Spain and, among other things, took an animated picture of a bull fight in Seville. This was tabooed in this country on the grounds that bull fighting was a cruel sport, and the pictures were not shown. After that I went to the North Cape to take pictures of the Midnight Sun. Films in those days were no longer than fifty feet. Difficulties in showing them were very great. There was always eight or ten breaks during a performance, and when gas was used there was always a good chance of its running short. When King Edward went to Ireland with Lord and Lady Dudley, I accompanied them throughout their tour and took animated pictures. I took the first pictures that had ever been taken of mountaineering in Switzerland, and soon afterwards I obtained a cinematograph record of the sinking of a ship. I was on board the Empress of Britain when she collided with the Helvetia and sank it. The film was put on at the Palace Theatre and ran continuously for six weeks.'

Variety audiences, entertained by these vastly-improved Bioscope reels at the end of an evening's comedy and song, could watch the world from their local theatre.

Dramas became more sophisticated, comedies more skilfully produced, and the Bioscope emerged as an entertainment force to be reckoned with. As an indication of its growing stature, many theatres began advertising Cine-Variety programmes to compete with the burgeoning kinemas. Film-making was approaching the scale of a production line, but the haste to feed the new market was not without mishap.

FRANK MOTTERSHAW, of the Sheffield Photo Company, one of the early British studios, had made one of the first chase movies in Derbyshire. *Daylight Burglary*, 400 feet long, was shown twenty times a day round the fairgrounds until it wore out. It cost £25 to produce and 500 copies were made, spurring on Mottershaw to greater things. One of the little publicized attractions of *Daylight Burglary* was that a real policeman had spotted the actor dressed as a burglar and grappled with the unfortunate man before leading him away in handcuffs – unaware that Mottershaw was filming the whole incident.

There were times when the unexpected became an occupational hazard: 'During some Scottish strike riots I had taken my film from a bridge,' Mottershaw said. 'The strikers accused me of exploiting them for making money. Things looked ugly, for they threatened to throw me and my camera into the river unless I handed over the film. I opened the camera and gave them a box of film which they fired. But it was the box of unexposed film. I have been arrested three times in the course of my occupation. Once in the Balkan States, once in Shireoaks, Notts., for trespassing on the railway line, and again in 1914 in Scarborough, the day after the bombardment. This incident began to look serious, as I was arrested by the military authorities on suspicion of having taken films showing the defences. I was handed over to the police, but I got them into telephonic communication with the Deputy Chief Constable of Sheffield who knew me.

'The police often made things very awkward for us. If they saw a kinema man inside the barriers on the occasion of a Royal visit, or any other important event, they would do their utmost to get him turned away. In 1905, when King Edward went to Liverpool to lay the foundation stone for the new university, I was in St George's Square when an angry inspector ordered me away. The King was looking towards me and beckoned the inspector to leave me alone. A reporter noted this, and the incident appeared in the evening paper. Whenever I ran up against any over-officious police official I showed him the cutting. It was very useful.

'It was nothing to have finished prints ready within two and a half hours of an event. The St Leger at Doncaster, for instance, I took for many years. It was 4.30 before we got back to Sheffield and the first print was on the 6.50 express to Leeds, and the second on the 7.20 to St Pancras, arriving 10.20 and shown at the Alhambra before eleven. This was done every year.'

In 1904, Mottershaw was commissioned to film the King of Serbia's coronation, and set out on the long trip to the Balkans with 3000 m (10,000 ft) of film. It was a popular part of the world for assassinations and officials, seeing his camera set up on the main procession route, thought that it was some sophisticated new weapon. After examining it, he was given every facility to film. The journey back was by mule over the Montenegro Mountains and through occupied Turkey, where he was arrested but talked his way to freedom. Mottershaw and other newsreel pioneers set many of the high standards achieved by today's television cameramen.

Gaumont moved into making their own drama films, and encountered similar technical hitches. One of their first achievements was an old chestnut called *Curfew*. In

the words of Lt-Col Broadhead: 'We thought we were adventuring boldly if we invested five pounds in a production; but for that sum we could rig up props and run to the luxury of stars. Some of the productions were masterpieces – if only because they were bad. *Curfew* was one outstanding work which cannot be forgotten. You know the story – if the curfew rang it meant doom to the lover's heroine, so to save his life she went into the belfry, swung from the clapper and prevented the bell from tolling. She suffered from her devotion, but not more so than our star performer. She was a hefty woman, but full of fire and determination to win through.

'We had rather spread ourselves out on the props, and with the help of the carpenter and a home-made spire, we made what was for the times a very fair scene. The crucial moment came when the leading lady had to spring at the clapper. She braced herself and went. Her aim was perfect and her grip secure; but what with her attack and weight, and the flimsiness of our contraption, the attempt to stop the ring was far too successful. The whole belfry came down, and the star fell with it, to our horror and consternation – until seeing that no harm was done, we, like the belfry, collapsed.'

THE GOLDEN age of the Bioscope arrived just before the war as imported American films began to tighten their grip on the market. Edison's prediction that 'whoever controls the motion picture industry controls the most powerful medium of influence over the people', was coming true. As war clouds rolled over Europe a fierce business battle broke out between British and American film-makers for domination of the industry. America had the advantage in producing raw film stock. This gave British film-makers problems

Plasterwork detail.

during the war years when celluloid – an ingredient in explosives-manufacture – was required for the war effort.

A poignant sequel to this intense competition came in the early years of peace when companies met at the Connaught Rooms to decide whether Britain should continue to make pictures or throw in the towel to the powerful American challenge. One of the speakers was Friese-Greene, penniless, unable to afford to renew his patents, and living on hand-outs from the new movie moguls. He rose to his feet to give an impassioned speech supporting British films then, as he concluded, collapsed in his chair and died. The man who had spent everything developing the tools of the industry had just 1s10d (9p) in his pocket. 'The greatest of them all was wheeled away on a hand-ambulance brought round by two police constables,' an observer wrote, 'while the great limousines purred at the kerb outside to bear away the august ones of the cinema industry.'

During Friese-Green's lifetime, the novelty attraction of the penny gaff and the fairground had come of age. Films of two hours and more were a greater challenge, opening up in redundant music halls. All this, of course, had not escaped the attention of the gritty empire-builders who controlled the variety circuits. The Stoll, Moss and McNaghten empires watched from the summit of the entertainment mountain to see which way the wind might change and made preparations to act accordingly.

They were not alone in their fears – as Edward VII's lively, almost informal reign drew to a close Britain was undergoing an unsettling social revolution. 'This American invasion; this radical government so unexpectedly returned at the general election . . . these cartoons of John Bull looking over a wall at a bull labelled Labour . . . this feverishness generally – what did it all mean?' asked one of the characters in Vita Sackville-West's *Edwardians*. 'Did it all mean they were riding for some smash? and would the smash, when it came, be constructive or destructive?' Hardly any aspect of life for both rich or poor had escaped the upheaval of the first few years of the twentieth century. The last millstones of Victorianism had all but disappeared; there was less of the old certainty as the times became faster and slicker; 'a certain taste was arising which tended to eliminate unnecessary objects.'

The new leaven had begun to rise before the turn of the century, sending cracks through centuries of somnolent social order. 'The great house, the church, the village and the labourers and the servants in their stations seemed to me a closed and complete social system,' H. G. Wells observed in *Tono-Bungay*. '. . . The country towns seemed mere collections of shops, marketing places for the tenantry . . . I thought this was the order of the whole world . . . It seemed to be in the divine order. That all this fine appearance was already sapped, that there were forces at work that might presently carry away all this elaborate social system had scarcely dawned upon me.'

IN THE rapidly developing world of entertainment, Sir Oswald Stoll, who controlled a vast theatrical empire, was finely tuned to public taste and enthusiastic about the Bioscope from its earliest days. (In 1904 he published *The Grand Survival: A Theory of Immortality by Natural Law*, an appropriate subject for a man whose business risks were legendary.) His fervent crusade was to create a mainstream of broad-based family entertainment for all classes. He saw Stoll theatres as entertainment centres where anyone could go for enjoyment without offence. It was partly a reaction against the rough music hall world from which he had climbed, but also a sense that the future lay in the widest possible public appeal. He vetted films shown at his Bioscope theatres before their

release, and brought into line the more outrageous variety turns; the most outrageous he declined to book. One of his methods of policing them was to issue all his theatre managers with a memo to file a report on any artist who used 'unseemly' language on his stages. He pursued it to the point of obsession, but saw that the bawdiness of Music Hall had a limited social appeal, and that Variety, too, might have it its limitations.

Stoll looked like a mild-mannered accountant against his larger-than-life cigar-smoking competitors in their fur-collared overcoats. He was not a conversationalist, but listened intently, fixing the speaker with a blank stare over his gold pince-nez. His business instincts were formidable, and when he made a decision he would fire someone rather than listen to their arguments. His weak spot was Vesta Tilley, with whom he was said to be secretly in love. Stoll wrote several of her songs and was furious when she married his business commercial rival Walter de Frece.

He was born in Australia, but when his father died his mother, Adelaide, returned to her native Liverpool where she married John Stoll, who ran a small local music hall. Oswald took his stepfather's name and acquired a lively, if inexperienced interest in the business. He was only fourteen when John Stoll died, and bravely squared up to the responsibility of running their Parthenon Assembly Rooms with his mother, who had always taken a back seat in management. Young Stoll soon found that, despite his enthusiasm, no one would take him seriously. In desperation he was forced to create a fictitious theatre manager to whom he relayed messages when striking deals. Amazingly few seemed to question why the man was never around, and none suspected that the boy was making all the decisions with his mother installed in the box office. The Parthenon continued to prosper, but even at that tender age his

Buxton Opera House.

quest for propriety had begun. Hannen Swaffer mentioned him locking patrons in their boxes at the side of the stage to prevent them tickling the legs of his dancing girls.

Stoll eventually made enough money to purchase a run-down Cardiff music hall – which he promptly renamed the Cardiff Empire – with Adelaide again manning the box office. The odd tradition continued throughout his empire building. When he built the £300,000 London Coliseum in 1904 – a magnificent Italian Renaissance theatre complete with tower and roof garden – Mrs Stoll was still loyally out front collecting the takings. The Coliseum was his crowning glory and a single-minded attempt to further his idea of family entertainment. It featured a £70,000 revolving stage to step up the pace of his shows by changing sets backstage ready for the next act. He also introduced an idea from America of three performances daily, which artists found gruelling, but it gave the Coliseum a name for instant entertainment. The public wanted non-stop action and Stoll was prepared to spend a fortune providing it.

What he failed to bargain for, however, was the quirky British concept of having a good time. Matinée audiences clearly felt uncomfortable watching Variety in the middle of the afternoon. There was an air of unease about the whole thing, rather like the way some people feel about watching television in the morning. They felt that Variety's rightful place was in the evening and, when the novelty began to fade, box office takings followed suit. Two years after its fanfare opening the Coliseum went bankrupt, indicating that Variety's dominance was not as unshakable as many thought. Dundas Slater, the theatre manager, was overcome by the financial disaster and shot himself through the head in a hansom cab outside the theatre. Stoll managed to reopen the Coliseum a year later with a safer mixture of Variety and straight

drama sketches by well-known West End actors. The new-look programme, and the emerging counter-attractions of the Bioscope were the first sign of changing preferences in entertainment. By 1919, he was expanding into the film industry, with interests both in studios and cinemas.

His great rival, Sir Edward Moss, who died in 1912, ran thirty-three theatres, the biggest single chain in the country. Moss's working life also began the hard way, travelling the country with a Diorama – a pre-cinema fairground show of moving rolls of painted canvas depicting scenes from the Franco-Prussian war. By the age of twenty-five the showman had his own music hall in Edinburgh. He acquired and commissioned theatres wherever he could find suitable sites, and in 1899, when his company had a £1,000,000 share value, he merged part of his interests with Stoll.

Cinema, by 1909, had finally blossomed enough to warrant the Cinematograph Act, aimed at tightning safety regulations in the hundreds of hurriedly-converted buildings sprouting across the country. Anyone wishing to show films had to apply for a licence and submit to regulations. It is an indication of the popularity of the movies that few variety theatres chose not to apply. Three Bioscope hall disasters had hastened the Act, the worst at Barnsley Public Hall where a cine-variety show was in progress. A rush for seats in a special children's performance resulted in a stampede in which eighteen were trampled underfoot and died. At Stratford, East London, equipment caught fire when a film jammed in the projector gate and the hall had to be evacuated. The operator, an inexperienced teenager, fled screaming when the machine burst into flames.

As the cinema grew, widening people's vision beyond a gas-lit stage, the curtain fell on music halls one by one. By the outbreak of World War I the great theatre-building boom, the most prolific in history, was over. In the golden years between 1896 and 1910 eighty-six new theatres had reared impressively on the drab skylines of cities and provincial towns. Sadly, only half of them are still in use; the rest lie derelict, but not beyond the bounds of restoration. Hundreds more, however, are lost forever; magnificent palaces of entertainment have been demolished to make way for supermarkets, ring roads, shopping developments, and other bland but necessary conveniences.

The Edwardian era was our greatest age of theatre construction; many were built by the prolific Frank Matcham for Stoll and Moss Empires. Their soaring auditoria cascaded with rich colours, gilt and marble statuary, crimson carpets, gleaming brass orchestra rails, dazzling chandeliers and potted palms; a warm and comforting intimacy which brought a welcome respite from mean streets and poor living. A handful, which includes Buxton Opera House, York Theatre Royal, the Hay-market, Newcastle Royal, Wyndhams and the Richmond Theatre, are still thriving. The sad death toll of other beautiful theatres has been shameful by any standards – of more than 1000 flourishing in the salad days of Variety in the years before World War I, 840 have been destroyed. The Society of Theatre Consultants and the Society for Theatre Research have worked heroically to breathe life into the few that remain. But even with the best resources and imaginative management prepared to adjust to changing times, nothing can be achieved without the support of audiences. Music Hall and Variety have gone, taking many of the great Empires, Alhambras and Palaces with them. All that remains of an important part of entertainment history are a few diminishing memories and some empty monuments – dust-blown, peeling and in need of repair. With the right will, many of our lost Empires could be put to good use again.

Anyone with an interest in the great days of Music Hall and Variety might wish to contact:

The British Music Hall Society,
Hon. Sec. Daphne Masterton,
c/o Brodie & Middleton,
68 Drury Lane,
London WC2.
Tel: 01-836 3289

Our theatre heritage is rapidly disappearing. The Society for Theatre Research provides a meeting point for all those interested in its history and technique. Enquiries should be addressed to:

The Society for Theatre Research,
77 Kinnerton Street,
London SW1X 3ED.

The Society of Theatre Consultants is a fully professional organization dedicated to renovating and preserving fine old theatres. The address of the secretary is:

The Society of Theatre Consultants,
4-7 Great Pulteney Street,
London W1R 3DF.
Tel: 01-434 3904

# ACKNOWLEDGMENTS

The author would like to acknowledge the help and co-operation of:

Granada Television; *Lost Empires* producer June Howson; director Alan Grint; magical advisor David Hemingway; stills photographer, Stuart Darby; John Woods; Nicky Cooney; Peter Mares; Jimmy Murphy of NYC; Geoff Mellor of the British Music Hall Society; Bob Dickinson for help with interviews; Bovis Construction Audio-Visual Dept.; British Rail Press Office; Manchester Studies; Mrs Blades, Mr Foy and the late Mr Marsden for their reminiscences.

The following publishers and International Music Publications for permission to reproduce the lyric quotations from the copyright songs as listed below.

*Chappell Music Ltd*
Your King & Country Needs You.

*Ascherberg, Hopwood & Crew Ltd*
We Don't Want To Fight; What Cheer 'Ria; The Blessings Of Marriage; Woman, Lovely Woman; The Lady Bicyclist; The Gay River; Waiting For The Turn Of The Tide.

*B. Feldman & Co Ltd*
The New Electric Light; Everybody's Doing It; Don't Go Out Tonight, Dear Father; The Cabman's Story; Alexander's Ragtime Band; A Stroke Of The Pen; He Was A Good Kind Husband; I Do Like To Be Beside The Seaside; Something In The Seaside Air; Playing The Game In The West.

*Francis, Day & Hunter Ltd*
At Trinity Church I Met My Doom; Waiting At The Church; They Didn't Believe Me; Take Me On The Flip Flap; The 7th Royal Fusiliers; What's That For, Eh?; Gilbert The Filbert; Fred Karnes Army; And The Verdict Was; At My Time Of Life; Poor John; The Army Of Today; She Was Poor But She Was Honest; I Shall Sleep Well Tonight; My Fiddle Is My Sweetheart; Mary Anne's Refused Me.

*Reynolds Music*
My Old Dutch; The Special Constable.

*West's Ltd*
There's A Long, Long Trail A-Winding.

The following publishers for permission to use quotations. Macmillan for the Earl of Stockton's *Winds Of Change*; Weidenfeld & Nicolson for Lord Olivier's *Confessions of an Actor*; Heinemann for J. B. Priestley's *Lost Empires* and George Rainbird for J. B. Priestley's *The Edwardians*; Robert Hale for Milbourne Christopher's *Illustrated History of Magic*; Martin, Secker & Warburg for John Fisher's *World of the Forsythes*; Virago Press Ltd for Vita Sackville-West's *The Edwardians*.

Sylvana Nown for researching the book, and patience beyond the call of duty. Extracts from pre-World War I newspapers and magazines are from Graham and Sylvana Nown's own collection.

The following for permission to reproduce photographs in which they hold the copyright. BBC Hulton Picture Library, page 13, 14, 15, 18, 27, 34, 51, 102, 103, 140, 142; Bovis Construction Ltd, page 144, 153; Granada TV, page 10, 12, 17, 20, 21, 30, 31, 32, 36, 37, 38, 39, 44, 46, 47, 48, 50, 52, 81, 82, 83, 98, 105, 110, 118, 119, 122, 127, 129, 151; Ronald Grant, page 40, 42, 56, 60, 109, 114, 120, 137; The Museum of London, endpapers; The Raymond Mander & Joe Mitchenson Theatre Collection, page 29, 69, 75, 77, 87, 93, 100, 106, 111, 132.

The author and publishers have made every effort to trace the copyright owners of extracts quoted in this book and apologize for omissions.